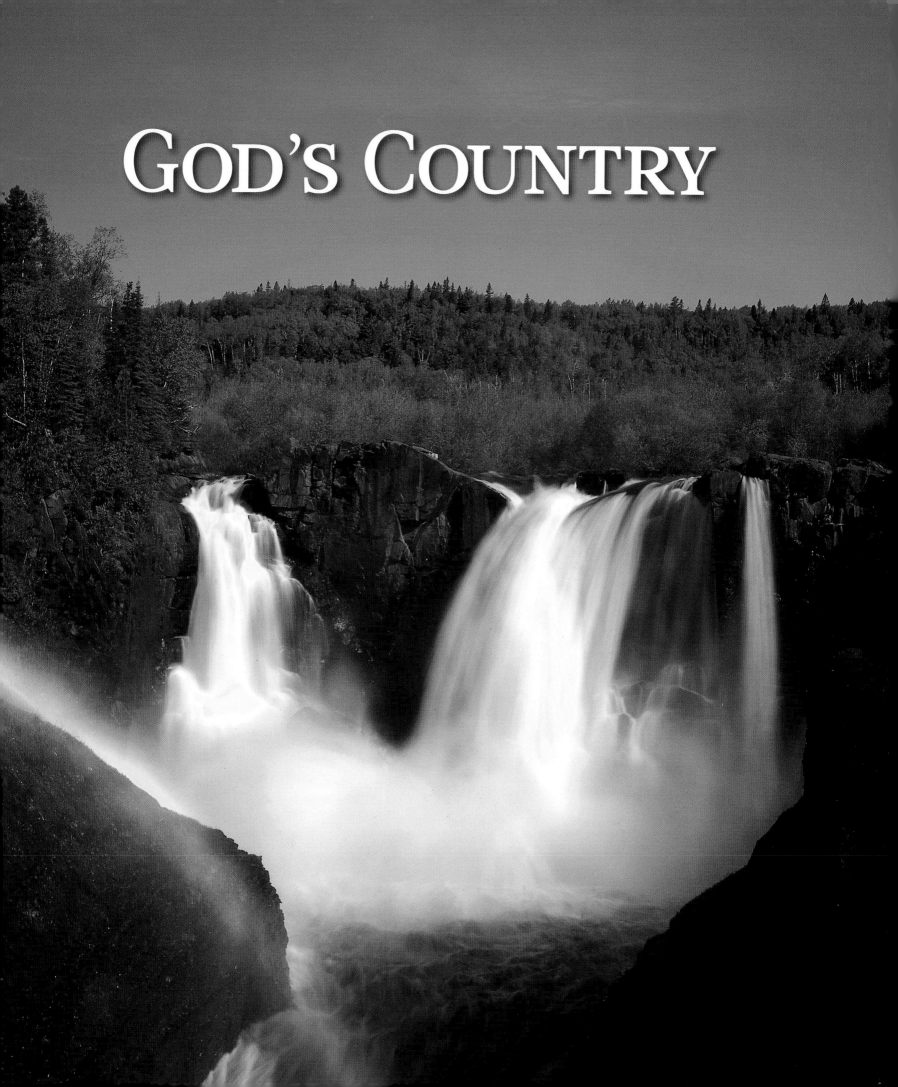

GOD'S COUNTRY

Editorial

EXECUTIVE EDITOR • *Heather Lamb*

CREATIVE DIRECTOR • *Howard Greenberg*

EDITORIAL OPERATIONS DIRECTOR • *Kerri Balliet*

ASSOCIATE CREATIVE DIRECTOR • *Sharon K. Nelson*

PROJECT EDITOR • *Lori Vanover*

CONTRIBUTING ART DIRECTOR • *Kristin Cleveland*

EDITOR, COUNTRY • *Robin Hoffman*

SENIOR EDITOR, COUNTRY • *John Burlingham*

ART DIRECTOR, COUNTRY • *Scott Schiller*

EDITORIAL ASSISTANT, COUNTRY • *Lorie L. West*

COPY CHIEF • *Deb Warlaumont Mulvey*

COPY EDITORS • *Joanne Weintraub, Dulcie Shoener*

CONTRIBUTING PROOFREADER • *Valerie Phillips*

EDITORIAL PRODUCTION MANAGER • *Dena Ahlers*

CONTRIBUTING LAYOUT DESIGNER • *Matt Fukuda*

DIGITAL EDITOR • *Jamieson Hawkins Krampf*

BUSINESS ANALYST • *Kristy Martin*

BILLING SPECIALIST • *Mary Ann Koebernik*

Business

VICE PRESIDENT, GROUP PUBLISHER
Russell S. Ellis

ASSOCIATE PUBLISHER
Chris Dolan

EAST COAST AND MIDWEST
Sabrina Ng • nysales@rd.com

WEST COAST
Catherine Marcussen • nysales@rd.com

DIRECT RESPONSE ADVERTISING
Jennifer Izzo • jizzo@mediapeople.com

ASSOCIATE MARKETING DIRECTOR, INTEGRATED SOLUTIONS
Katie Gaon

VICE PRESIDENT, BRAND MARKETING
Jennifer Smith

VICE PRESIDENT, CIRCULATION AND CONTINUITY MARKETING
Dave Fiegel

MARKETING DIRECTOR
Christina Masterson

ART DIRECTOR
Ed Jackson

MARKETING MANAGER
Carolyn Yanoff

MARKETING COORDINATOR
Amanda Gottlieb

ADVERTISING PRODUCTION MANAGER
Lisa Becker

Reader's Digest North America

VICE PRESIDENT, BUSINESS DEVELOPMENT AND MARKETING
Alain Begun

PRESIDENT, BOOKS AND HOME ENTERTAINMENT
Harold Clarke

GENERAL MANAGER, CANADA
Philippe Cloutier

VICE PRESIDENT, OPERATIONS
Mitch Cooper

CHIEF OPERATING OFFICER
Howard Halligan

VICE PRESIDENT, CHIEF SALES OFFICER
Mark Josephson

VICE PRESIDENT, GENERAL MANAGER, MILWAUKEE
Frank Quigley

VICE PRESIDENT, DIGITAL SALES
Steve Sottile

VICE PRESIDENT, CHIEF CONTENT OFFICER
Liz Vaccariello

VICE PRESIDENT, GLOBAL FINANCIAL PLANNING
Devin White

The Reader's Digest Association, Inc.

PRESIDENT AND CHIEF EXECUTIVE OFFICER
Robert E. Guth

International Standard Book Number (13):
978-1-61765-244-8
Component Number:
116200051H

Library of Congress Control Number: 2013933812

All rights reserved. Printed U.S.A.

FOR QUESTIONS OR TO ORDER ADDITIONAL COPIES:
Call toll-free: 800-880-3012
Visit: shoptasteofhome.com/country or country-magazine.com

© 2013 Reiman Media Group, Inc.
5400 S. 60th St., Greendale WI 53129-1404

Cover: Wildflower meadow in the San Juan Mountains, Colorado
PHOTO BY MARY LIZ AUSTIN

Front pages: Coastline of Gros Morne National Park in Newfoundland
PHOTO BY JOHN SYLVESTER

Previous page: Roaring High Falls of the Pigeon River on the Minnesota-Canada border
PHOTO BY BOB FIRTH

Facing page: Farmstead near York, Nebraska
PHOTO BY GREG LATZA

Back pages: Sunrise over Resurrection Bay, Seward, Alaska
PHOTO BY RON NIEBRUGGE

When I imagine God's Country, I see snow-draped mountain peaks,

hardwood forests and babbling brooks. These are the places that make my heart soar. But my wife, Kathy, soars at the seashore. My cousin Don hears angels sing when he gazes across the parched deserts of Southern California. Our ace copy editor Dulcie gets all misty-eyed over scenes like this one from the prairies of her native Nebraska. As they talk about these places, their voices dance. Their eyes shine. And they cast the lands they love in an enticing new light.

That's the amazing journey you're about to take thanks to editor Lori Vanover, designer Kristin Cleveland and some of the finest scenic photographers in North America. This book highlights 13 of the nearly 140 God's Country stories that have graced *Country* and *Country Extra* over the last 23 years—plus two wonderful new stories about the Great Plains and Alaska. These are some of our all-time favorite stories, but we don't intend them as a "best of" collection, because as Lori says, "God's Country means something different to each of us, and that's the best part."

Think of it as a chance to travel through 15 of the continent's friendliest, most fascinating, most spectacular places alongside the people who know and love them best. Then let your heart soar.

ROBIN HOFFMAN, *COUNTRY* EDITOR

GOD'S

Map illustrations by Scott Schille

COUNTRY

Newfoundland and Labrador

Minnesota's Arrowhead Region

Georgian Bay

New York

Great Plains

Northern Illinois

Pennsylvania

Blue Ridge Region

Kentucky

Texas Rolling Plains

Southeast Coast

ATLANTIC OCEAN

GULF of MEXICO

EAST

The Northeast's rich history ranges from colorful coastal fishing villages to family farms that have graced the land for centuries. Each mile tells the stories of people who paved a path forward.

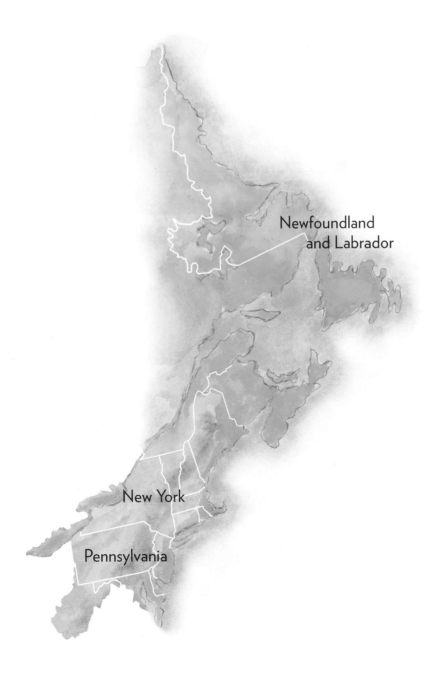

Newfoundland and Labrador

New York

Pennsylvania

Newfoundland and Labrador's rugged beauty and friendly people captured his heart.

Story and photos by JOHN SYLVESTER

My love affair with Newfoundland and Labrador began more than 25 years ago, when a friend and I spent a two-week summer vacation exploring Canada's easternmost province by car. Our journey began with a six-hour ferry trip from North Sydney, Nova Scotia, across the Strait of Canso to Port aux Basques on the island of Newfoundland.

On board we were immediately befriended by a crew of Newfoundland fishermen bound for home after several weeks at sea. They regaled us with stories of their life at sea and of their island home. It was a fitting introduction. This is a place of breathtaking natural beauty, from the soaring peaks of Labrador's Torngat Mountains to the rugged coastline of the Avalon Peninsula. You'll see drifting icebergs, breaching whales, and countless seabirds and picturesque fishing villages.

You'll also meet extraordinarily warmhearted, friendly people who are quick of wit and always ready with a story. I soon learned that if I stopped to ask for directions, I should expect a lengthy, but always engaging, conversation.

Newfoundland and Labrador is one province but two distinct places. About 98 percent of the province's 510,000 people live on the island of Newfoundland, affectionately referred to as "The Rock" by residents.

In addition to the main island, more than 5,000 smaller islands dot the province's 18,020 miles of rocky coastline. The capital, St. John's, is the easternmost city in North America.

Labrador is part of Canada's mainland, separated from

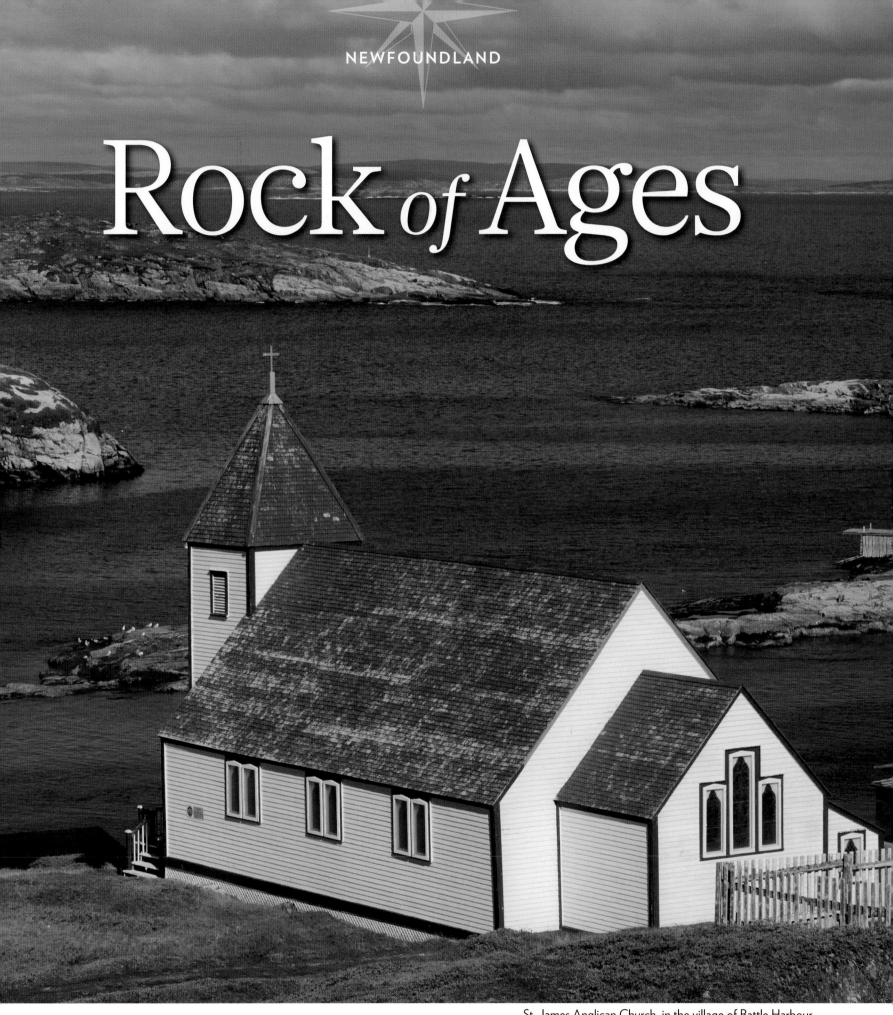

Rock *of* Ages

St. James Anglican Church, in the village of Battle Harbour

Joseph and Jenny Merkuratsuk in the remote village of Hebron, Labrador

Northern gannets at Cape St. Mary's Ecological Preserve

A curious caribou on the Avalon Peninsula

Doris Roberts and her homemade bread at Quirpon Island Lighthouse Inn

Crab fishermen on the Petty Harbour wharf near St. John's

Newfoundland by the Strait of Belle Isle, a channel about 80 miles long and 12 miles wide that flows between the Gulf of St. Lawrence and the Atlantic Ocean. The province covers about 156,000 square miles, making it larger than all but three states in the U.S.

Newfoundland and Labrador was a British colony until it joined Canada in 1949, and it was called simply Newfoundland until 2001. But its remarkable human history dates back more than 9,000 years, when indigenous peoples roamed its land. Their descendants, the Inuit, inhabit Labrador's northern territory, which they call Nunatsiavut—"Our Beautiful Land."

The first Europeans arrived about 1,000 years ago when Vikings attempted a settlement on the northern tip of the island. It didn't survive, however, and it wasn't until French and British colonists arrived in the late 1500s that settlement finally took hold.

Today's residents can trace their lineage back to those early settlers, and accents of French, Irish and English can still be heard in their voices. In fact, the accents can be so strong that, depending on where you are, you might think you're in Ireland, the west country of England, or listening to another language altogether! I've had many an embarrassing moment trying to decipher the dialect I was hearing.

Newfoundland and Labrador is a place defined by the sea.

A friendly neighborhood sheep in Gros Morne National Park

It's a place where "fish" meant cod: For more than 400 years the people relied on cod for their livelihood, venturing out in small boats from hundreds of tiny communities that hugged the coastline.

On that first summer vacation trip to Newfoundland, I pitched my tent on a hillside overlooking the idyllic fishing village of New Bonaventure and awoke to the sound of screen doors slapping. I poked my head out of the tent to the sight of fishermen ambling down narrow lanes to their boats.

My friend and I scrambled out of our sleeping bags and hurried down to the wharf, where we were immediately invited to join two fishermen as they checked their elaborate fishing nets, called cod traps.

We spent a lovely morning on the water watching those hardy men of the sea haul cod from their traps. Bald eagles also kept a careful eye on their progress from atop spruce trees lining the gray oceanside cliffs.

While the cod fishery has fallen on hard times in recent years

and coastal towns and villages are shrinking, some are finding new life as destinations for travelers searching for peace, quiet and unspoiled natural beauty. Hollywood even came calling to New Bonaventure: Years after my first visit, the little village was selected as the location for the filming of the 2001 movie *The Shipping News*, based on Annie Proulx's Pulitzer Prize-winning novel.

While I seem to discover a new favorite place with each visit to Newfoundland and Labrador, there are a few that I return to again and again. Gros Morne National Park on the island's west coast is one such place. A hiker's paradise, it encompasses a large section of the Long Range Mountains, an outer range of the Appalachians. Gros Morne, the mountain for which the park is named, stands alone overlooking Bonne Bay. It is the province's second-highest peak at 2,644 feet. A hike to the top of Gros Morne is a must for every park visitor.

On one memorable visit, I rose early, donned backpack and headlamp and set out to reach the summit by sunrise, hoping

Calved from the Greenland ice cap, these behemoths drift south along the coast from April to August.

Parade of icebergs in Notre Dame Bay in the village of Hart's Cove

Polar bear on Labrador's rocky north coast

to photograph the view from the mountaintop in the early-morning light. My trek began under starry skies, but by the time I reached the top, it was completely enshrouded in fog. I could barely see the ground beneath my feet, and I feared I'd hiked a long way for nothing.

But just as quickly as it came, the fog lifted, revealing a breathtaking view of the neighboring mountains. And in the valley below, the blue waters of Ten Mile Pond glittered in the soft morning sunlight.

With their typical flair for understatement, Newfoundlanders name their lakes "ponds." They also named an 800-foot waterfall Rattling Brook!

Place-names in Newfoundland and Labrador are as colorful as the people who live there. Heart's Delight, Little Heart's Ease, Billy Butts Pond, Toogood Arm, Joe Batt's Arm, Quidi Vidi (pronounced "kiddy viddy") and Tickle Cove are just a few.

With language that interesting, there's an entire book, *The Dictionary of Newfoundland English*, to help you with some of the terms. It defines tickle, for example, as a "narrow difficult strait" between islands.

One of the main attractions for many visitors, especially photographers, is the parade of icebergs that drifts past each spring. Calved from the Greenland ice cap, these behemoths of 10,000-year-old glacial ice drift south along the coast from April to August.

While your chances of seeing icebergs from the shore are very good, I prefer to take a boat tour or hire a fisherman to take me out on the water to photograph the 'bergs up close.

A few years back, during one especially good iceberg season, I traveled to Twillingate, the self-proclaimed "Iceberg Capital of the World." I asked the proprietor of the bed-and-breakfast where I was staying if she could recommend someone to take me by boat so that I could photograph in the evening light.

"Oh, my daughter's boyfriend has a boat," she offered. "I'll give him a call." A few hours later, 18-year-old Keith and I were skimming over the calm waters of Notre Dame Bay in his small outboard-powered dory.

It was a lovely evening, and I was delighted to photograph several beautifully sculpted icebergs bathed in warm sunset light. Each time we moved the boat, I asked Keith to cut the engine to reduce vibration while I photographed. He happily

Fortune Head Lighthouse on the Burin Peninsula

Fancifully sculpted icebergs off the coast of Quirpon Island

obliged, but he then had to restart the engine each time by repeatedly pulling the starter cord, eventually pulling the cord right out of the engine!

"Not to worry," he said. And without a word of complaint, he started rowing—and telling stories. I especially remember how proudly he spoke of his grandfather, who still cut his own firewood with a hand saw, because a chain saw wastes wood.

Later that evening, when I finally arrived back at the bed-and-breakfast, my hosts offered me a traditional Newfoundland nightcap: a glass of rum with iceberg ice in it. The ice popped and fizzed in my drink as 10,000-year-old air bubbles escaped. These are the kind of good times—and good people—you never want to forget.

One recent spring I returned to Notre Dame Bay to photograph icebergs near Fogo Island and the Change Islands. I'd been to Fogo before, but I was visiting Change Islands for the first time.

From the moment I left the dock of the small car ferry that connects the two islands, I had the feeling I was stepping back in time. Saltbox houses perched on cliffs overlooking tidy fish sheds and stages (wooden wharves), where brightly painted wooden boats cast reflections in the water. There's even a general store without a sign to mark its location. After all, everyone knows where it is!

I booked a room at the island's only inn, whose owner—a diminutive grandmother in her 70s—warmly greeted me. It was early in the season, so I was the only guest. At breakfast she served her homemade partridgeberry jam, a Newfoundland specialty. It was the best I'd ever tasted, and I told her so.

The next morning a full jar of jam landed on the breakfast table for me to take home. And when I'd finished that jar, my host told me, I was to call her for more. She said her son was a commercial pilot, and she'd send another jar of jam with him when he flew to my province.

I never tested her generosity, nor her son's, but it was another example of the exceptional warmth and hospitality that keeps me coming back to God's Country. ✳

Backroads to Tranquility

An Amish farm nestled in rolling fields near East Randolph

Idyllic treasures await those who venture beyond the Big Apple.

Story and photos by ROBERT OLEJNICZAK

Between the towering skyscrapers of New York City and the thundering waters of Niagara Falls lie thousands of miles of rural highways and back roads that wind their way through small towns, forests and farmland. This is the part of New York that I like to call God's Country.

Quiet country life is evident in my hometown of East Randolph, where you'll likely find an Amish buggy tied to the hitching post at the local hardware store. Our Amish neighbors warmly welcome visitors to browse their shops, but there are no billboards along the highway promoting their wares.

The best way to see their handcrafted goods is to arm yourself with a good county map and find a knowledgeable local resident to point you down the right road. Hand-painted signs along the way will direct you to quilt shops, toys, baked goods, custom furniture, rugs, farm products and more.

Summer sees Amish farmers and their teams of horses working hard in the fields. In August, oats are shocked in preparation for harvest. Corn shocks appear a little later.

In the morning, milk cans stand alongside the road, waiting to be collected and their creamy contents made into locally produced cheeses.

Farming is not limited to the Amish, however. Modern agriculture thrives in the Empire State. Our dairy industry is the third largest in U.S. milk production and ranks first in cream cheese and cottage cheese production.

Many roadside produce stands attest to New York's status as

Amish buggies at a worship service, held in members' homes

a leading producer of apples, cauliflower, onions, pears, snap beans and sweet corn.

The glacier-carved shores of Lake Erie, Lake Ontario and the Finger Lakes provide an ideal environment for grape production. Vineyards cover more than 36,000 acres, and a drive through the region awakens the senses at harvesttime. The fruity scent of ripening grapes perfumes the countryside.

Back when I was an apartment dweller, I considered nearby Allegany State Park my backyard. With three quiet lakes (no motorized vessels allowed), more than 60,000 acres of forest, 90 miles of hiking, biking and horseback trails and an abundance of wildlife, Allegany has been one of my favorite places to enjoy God's creation.

New York offers a variety of waterways for boaters and fishermen. While larger vessels cruise the Great Lakes and other major lakes in the state, paddlers are especially fond of the hundreds of smaller ponds and streams, which offer quiet days of exploration and wildlife viewing. More adventuresome

rafters and kayakers might try taming the rugged whitewater of the Zoar Valley, Hudson River, Letchworth Gorge and Sacandaga River. Some 90 species of fish can be found in these waterways, including perch, trout, walleye, muskellunge, bass, salmon and northern pike.

As frequently as possible, I head north to the rivers, forests and mountains of Adirondack Park. The "park" is actually a patchwork of 6 million acres of public and private lands, which are designated by the state constitution to be "forever wild."

In summer, I am particularly drawn to the area's miles of hiking trails. I enjoy the solitude of long walks through the forest and steep climbs up mountainsides, which still continue to surprise me with awe-inspiring views, unexpected waterfalls and unparalleled tranquility. There's nowhere I'd rather be, feeling close to God as I stand in humility and amazement at the creation of His hand.

I also never miss the arrival of autumn in the Adirondacks—though each season in the Adirondacks has its own unique

The west branch of the Ausable River in the Adirondacks High Peaks region

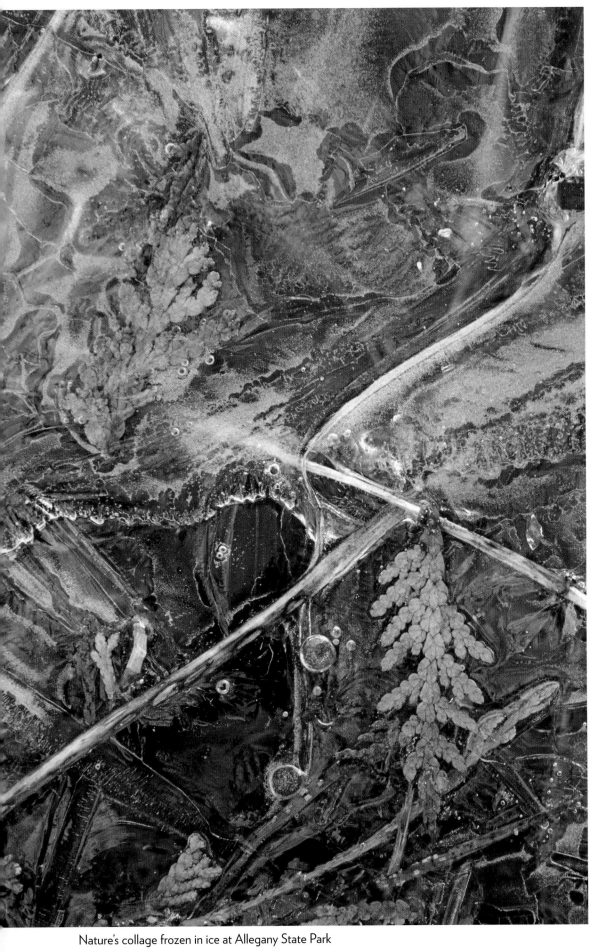

Nature's collage frozen in ice at Allegany State Park

Birches at Chapel Pond, southeast of Lake Placid

Concord grapes in a Finger Lakes vineyard

The simple charms of spring in Chautauqua County

Going eye to eye with a green frog

A typical pastoral scene along an Adirondacks back road

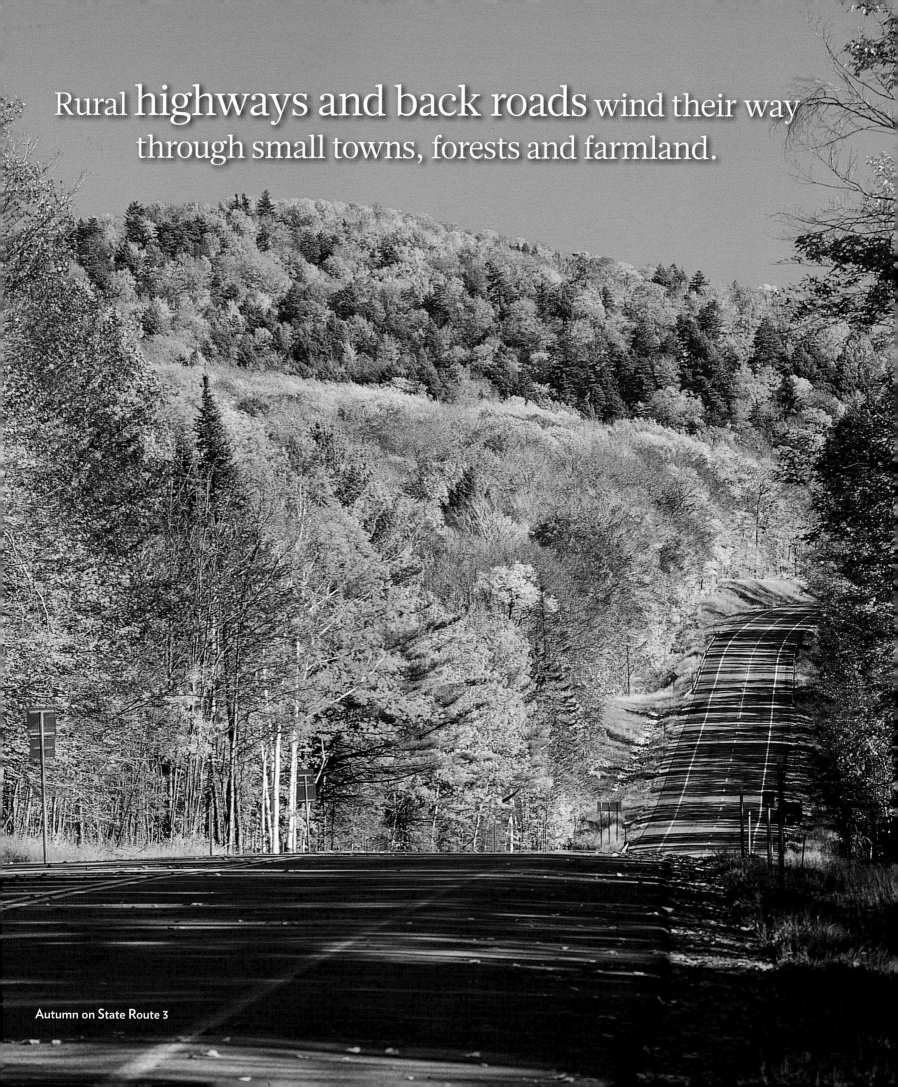

Rural highways and back roads wind their way through small towns, forests and farmland.

Autumn on State Route 3

A curious chipmunk alongside an Adirondacks stream

charm. The fall foliage of the High Peaks region in northeastern New York is an absolute paradise for a photographer seeking brilliantly colorful landscapes. Peak foliage colors come early this far north. The leaves begin to change in late September, usually peaking in the first days of October.

The mix of evergreens and hardwoods on the mountainsides offers a striking contrast in colors that draws tourists and photographers from around the world. Maples burst with vibrant reds and oranges, while the birches and beeches glow in every shade of yellow against a background of green pines.

Just south of the Adirondacks, the Catskill Mountains are sometimes called America's First Wilderness because scholars note the environmental conservation movement started here. Its rugged beauty continues to draw hikers and climbers to spectacular sights such as 260-foot-high Kaaterskill Falls.

Wildlife abounds in upstate New York. White-tailed deer are a common sight, along with smaller animals like opossums, raccoons and porcupines. Wild turkeys can sometimes be seen along the back roads or in fields in the early morning.

Black bears are making a comeback. Occasionally, in the early spring, I'll catch a glimpse of a young cub in the nearby hills. And the sight of a bald eagle is particularly exciting.

I must admit I've never visited the Big Apple, and I rarely join the crowds to view Niagara Falls. I'm content to munch on apples from a local orchard as I explore the quiet countryside between these two famous locations.

Why go to the big city when you can spend your time exploring the backroads in God's Country? ✳

Lucifer Falls in the upper gorge of Robert H. Treman State Park

Crisscrossing the countryside on back roads is the best route to Pennsylvania's rich heritage.

Story and photos by JERRY IRWIN

If I had just one word to describe Pennsylvania, that word would be valleys.

The topography consists of many soft green valleys created by the Appalachian, Allegheny and Blue Ridge mountains, which sweep diagonally, ridge after ridge, from the southwest to the northeast corners of the state.

I was born and raised in Pennsylvania and lived in Lancaster County for many years. Although I recently moved to Delaware, I still consider Pennsylvania my home. In fact, I live just 100 yards from the border and can walk there anytime I want. As far as I'm concerned, Pennsylvania is God's Country, and you won't find me straying too far away from it.

The valleys in the south-central part of the state are endowed with rich soil, making agriculture an important industry. In fact, the land supports one of the highest concentrations of small, family-owned farms in the country.

These farms, many of them Amish, average 70 acres. But don't dismiss them because of their relatively small size—they are highly productive.

Many of the older German farming settlements in this area date back more than 275 years. Lancaster County, which boasts some of the most productive and beautiful farmland on Earth, is considered a national treasure by many people.

Dense hardwood and conifer forests cover the other half of the state's land. More than 50 natural lakes and 45,000 miles of rivers and streams add to the tranquility and beauty.

Patchwork of Simple Pleasures

A bird's-eye view of Lancaster County in springtime

Retired farmers Lloyd and Virginia Weaver, who invite visitors to enjoy their thousands of tulips (right)

Leisurely canoe trip through the Brandywine River in Chester County (below)

Life in the slow lane along a winding Berks County back road (opposite)

While folks in a hurry take the Pennsylvania Turnpike to whiz across the state, I prefer the back roads, where the only traffic jams come from farmers driving their cows down the road. That's how to see Pennsylvania up close. On one photo-gathering assignment, I traveled 5,000 miles and never left the state's borders.

One of my favorite drives is Route 6, a 310-mile stretch of road without a foot of superhighway or interstate along its length. It winds its way through small towns and some of the most remote and sparsely populated areas of north-central and northeastern Pennsylvania.

As I've crisscrossed the state, I've gained an appreciation for the sturdy old barns that dot the landscape, including the classic Pennsylvania bank barns and others made of native fieldstones. They are often adorned with colorful hex signs, which some believe were originally intended to ward off evil spirits but now add to the charm of the countryside.

The post-and-beam construction of these 18th- and 19th-

I prefer the back roads, where the only traffic jams come from farmers driving their cows down the road.

A pretty church perched invitingly on a hillside in Susquehanna County

The continued tradition of decorated barns in Berks County

The expansive Pine Creek Gorge, also known as Pennsylvania's Grand Canyon

A bucolic German farmstead and covered bridge in Lancaster County

Amish children at play during a break from schoolwork

century masterpieces was patterned after the techniques used to build the great sailing ships of the day. I marvel at the labor it must have taken to raise them without modern power tools.

My backroads trips sometimes lead me to diverse community festivals that celebrate the German and other ethnic heritages of the state. There are farm auctions, too, with a couple hundred people showing up for the lively bidding, good food and fellowship.

And, of course, you never know when you'll discover a covered bridge around the next bend in the road. Pennsylvania has more than 200 of these inviting spans, the most of any state. Built in the 1800s, the bridges are a worthy testimony to old-fashioned craftsmanship and to a time when life was lived in the slow lane.

One of my most memorable experiences was a day in May when I surveyed the patchwork fields of Lancaster County from the window of a small Cessna airplane. Amish and Mennonite farmers were working the land with their teams of horses and mules. Some teams consisted of as many as seven animals in harness together.

Even from high in the air, I could smell the distinctive scent of the freshly tilled soil as I passed overhead. What a glorious time it was!

But then again, divine times like these are not uncommon in Pennsylvania. After all, this is God's Country. ✳

SOUTH

The pace of life traditionally moves a little slower here, which gives folks more time to appreciate all the warmth, authentic flavor and scenic grandeur the South has to offer.

Kentucky

Blue Ridge Region

Southeast Coast

Heart *of the* Hills

A farm tucked into the Blue Ridge landscape near Raphine, Virginia

They found love and a rewarding life in the mountains and valleys of the Blue Ridge.

Story and photos by PAT AND CHUCK BLACKLEY

We are blessed to have lived in the Blue Ridge Mountains all of our lives. In fact, our life together literally began on the Blue Ridge Parkway, for it was at one of its lofty overlooks that we became engaged. Some 40 years of marriage later, we're still roaming these mountains. We've traveled all over the country, but no other place speaks to our hearts like the Blue Ridge, for this truly is God's Country.

The Blue Ridge Range is actually the easternmost ridge of the southern Appalachian Mountains. The range begins in southern Pennsylvania and stretches approximately 500 miles, ending in northern Georgia. The Appalachians are among the most ancient mountains in the world, and once towered as high as the Rockies. All the years of weathering have worn down those once-rugged peaks to gentle ridges that average 3,000 to 4,000 feet around our home in the Shenandoah Valley, and rise to 6,684 feet at their highest elevation, in North Carolina.

Although cities are fun to visit occasionally, we're small-town folk through and through. So the easy lifestyle here in the heart of Virginia's Blue Ridge suits us just fine. Our home is just a stone's throw from the southern entrance to Shenandoah National Park. We spend countless hours there, hiking in the mountains and photographing the flora and fauna.

Occasionally, we'll head up to the northern entrance of the park at Front Royal and drive south along the 105-mile Skyline Drive to Waynesboro. From there, we can continue along the 469-mile Blue Ridge Parkway all the way to Great Smoky

A farmer hauling silage for his cattle in Rockingham County, Virginia

Mountains National Park in North Carolina and Tennessee. And we can travel all that way without one stoplight or tractor-trailer truck—just hundreds of miles of peacefully pristine mountain scenery.

On each trip, we spend time in different towns and communities along the way, and we've concluded, without a doubt, that the people of the Blue Ridge are the warmest, friendliest folks you'll ever meet. They'll greet you, feed you, entertain you and send you on your way with a smile. People often stop to chat with us, and we frequently get tips on other intriguing places to photograph like an old mill or a farm with a particularly handsome barn.

The first Europeans to settle in the Blue Ridge region began arriving in the early 1700s. They were primarily Scotch-Irish, German and English, and those ancestral roots still run deep in the area. This heritage is expressed in the food and crafts you'll

Prime time for apple harvest in Frederick County, Virginia

People of the Blue Ridge are
the warmest, **friendliest folks** you'll ever meet.

Linn Cove viaduct on the Blue Ridge Parkway in North Carolina

A horse pull contest at the Blue Ridge Folklife Festival in Ferrum, Virginia

encounter along the way, as well as the music you'll hear. Listen closely to the traditional "mountain" music, and it will clearly remind you of Irish jigs and ballads.

Like their forefathers, many Blue Ridge residents still make their living from the land, thanks to our moderate climate, rich soil and abundant rainfall. Farms, both large and small, dot the landscape throughout the region.

But nowhere are they more abundant than in Virginia's famed Shenandoah Valley. This fertile stretch of land, which lies nestled between the mountain ridges, was called the "Breadbasket of the Confederacy" during the Civil War.

A drive through the rolling Shenandoah countryside reveals picturesque farms with barns, silos and farmhouses dating back 100 years or more. Many of those farms have remained in the same family the entire time.

Almost any weekend, you'll find some type of festival taking place in the Blue Ridge. In spring, there are dogwood, apple blossom, azalea, rhododendron and mountain laurel festivals. Summer brings celebrations for all types of berries, tomatoes, watermelons, cherries and peaches. Then there are the fall harvest festivals for grapes, apples and pumpkins.

Apple harvest season is especially ripe with celebrations, since this is a large apple-growing region. If you attend one of these festivals, you can sample, purchase or just watch the making of every yummy apple product imaginable—apple butter, cider, dumplings, fritters, pie, cake, jelly and candy. If it can be made from apples, you'll find it here!

But what we love most about the Blue Ridge is its abundance

Autumn splendor of Goshen Pass reflected in the Maury River in Rockbridge County, Virgina

Sherando Lake painted by brilliant fall foliage in Augusta County, Virginia

A white-tailed fawn with plenty to graze on in Shenandoah National Park

An old Farmall with a patriotic twist at a market in Deep Gap, North Carolina

A pleasant porch at a general store in Rockingham County, Virginia

Riders enjoying the peaceful rolling hills of North Carolina's Moses H. Cone Memorial Park

Bass Lake geese scouting for a meal near Blowing Rock, North Carolina

of natural beauty. And we are most fortunate to have so many public lands, parks and national forests that provide easy access to it. There are more public hiking trails than we could hike in a lifetime—trails that lead to breathtaking vistas, natural gardens, deep mysterious gorges or tumbling waterfalls. These natural areas provide abundant opportunities for wildlife watching, particularly deer, black bear, turkey, fox, bobcat, raccoon and many bird species.

The streams and rivers run clear and fast and are loaded with trout. Here we can fish, canoe, camp, backpack or swim—or simply relax and enjoy the solitude.

We could write a book about all that makes the Blue Ridge a special and alluring place. But we think William Bake summed it up nicely in his book *The Blue Ridge*. He wrote, "This is good country...both savage and gentle, grand and subtle—country given to life." In other words, this is God's Country! ✳

Mountain musicians in a toe-tapping jam session at a Blue Ridge fall festival

Golden light and a gorgeous view from a Skyline Drive overlook in Virginia's Shenandoah National Park

A paradise of verdant lands and lush history is just an exit away on the Southeast Coast.

Story by JOE GIBBONS • *Photos by* JOE AND BECKY GIBBONS

Horns honked! Tires squealed! Cars sped down the crowded highway like runaway trains. You'd think somebody up ahead was giving away gasoline, though my wife, Becky, and I knew better.

It was just another day in the maddening rush of Georgia's I-95. We were headed home to Florida, and it appeared that this trip would go no differently than it always had.

Then suddenly, we had a stroke of what turned out to be terrific luck: a traffic jam!

Most days, a multihour delay isn't what we'd consider good luck. However, this apparent misfortune would lead us to a region so beautiful, it could only be called God's Country.

Frustrated by the gridlock as well as the view of cones, cranes and construction, we decided to pull off at the next exit and find a place for the night. What we found was miles of lush, lime-green marshlands stretching as far as the eye could see. A still river snaked through the grasses as rays from the setting sun cast a bronze glow on a distant cable bridge.

"I don't know where 'there' is, but I know we're staying there," I told Becky, who eagerly agreed. It turned out we'd wandered onto a series of barrier islands that protect Georgia's coastline from destructive hurricanes. We chose to spend the night on Jekyll Island, and by the time we reached our destination, the sun had just begun to sink.

A glowing reddish hue painted the clouds, warmed the sky and glinted off the calm waters. Silhouetted oak trees reached

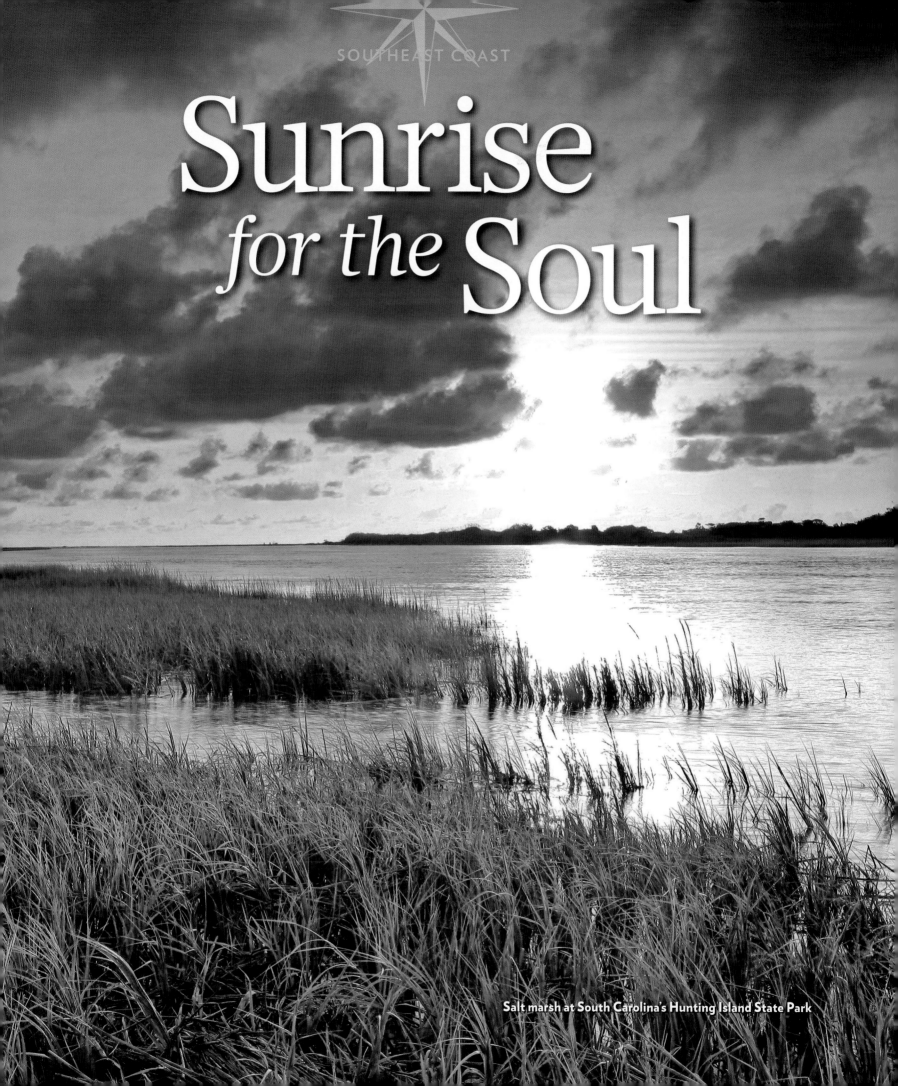

Sunrise
for the Soul

Salt marsh at South Carolina's Hunting Island State Park

Soft light on a stone angel in Oak Grove Cemetery, St. Marys, Georgia

First Presbyterian Church in St. Marys, Georgia's second-oldest church

out for each other's touch, almost dancing in the shadow of the soft light. At that moment, we realized that paradise just might be an exit off the interstate.

Before we left Jekyll Island, we discovered 10 miles of unspoiled beaches with uprooted oak and pine trees resting along its north side. A small community of homes and historic ruins gracefully shared the natural beauty.

After this eye-opening experience, we couldn't wait to explore more of the Southeast Coast.

We started in our home state of Florida and quickly discovered the Panhandle town of St. Marks. In the 1820s, this town was considered a vital port of entry for the planting and growing regions in Florida and Georgia.

These days, this small community (population 315) is known for bordering St. Marks National Wildlife Refuge, one of the nation's oldest and most beautiful wildlife refuges.

Pristine coastal marshes, tidal creeks and upland forests gave

us a look at an unspoiled Florida, where peace and quiet reign. More than 200 species of birds call St. Marks home, giving it the nickname "Birder's Paradise." Other residents include the Florida black bear, white-tailed deer, otters and raccoons.

After a great day of hiking, we watched the sunset near picturesque St. Marks Lighthouse, overlooking miles of marsh and sandy beach.

Farther down Florida's west coast, off bustling I-75, we discovered another beautiful surprise. Sanibel Island and Captiva Island are known for miles of scenic coastline, though seashells are their greatest claim to fame.

After a typical Florida thunderstorm, more than 250 kinds of shells wash onto the beach, transforming it into a colorful collage of sea treasures. Before we knew it, we'd joined our fellow beachgoers in the ritual "Sanibel stoop," roaming the beach and picking up shells.

A trip across the state took us to "space coast," a section of

Oyster shell concrete (or tabby) walls of South Carolina's St. Helena's Chapel of Ease, destroyed in an 1886 fire

Florida's east coast that's home to the Kennedy Space Center. The center is open for tours, and we timed it just right. We got to watch a shuttle liftoff from the beach!

Cocoa Beach, just up the road, was the setting for the 1960s sitcom *I Dream of Jeannie* (even though only one episode was actually filmed here). The area seems to offer something for everyone, drawing both retirees and young families alike.

Traveling north, we enjoyed family-friendly New Smyrna Beach and pet-friendly Smyrna Dunes Park. For a faster-paced experience, Daytona Beach beckons a few miles up the coast.

St. Augustine, the oldest city in North America, was our final stop in Florida. The Timucuan Indians once lived here. Then the Spanish, British and finally the United States shaped its growth.

Shops, bed-and-breakfasts and warm smiles welcomed us into a fascinating history that includes the Fountain of Youth, the Mission of Nombre de Dios and the Castillo de San Marcos, a 330-year-old, Spanish-built fortress never defeated in battle.

Family-oriented St. Augustine has frequent festivals, boating on the Intracoastal Waterway, majestic Casa Monica Hotel and historic Flagler College. The old city also has a sweet, romantic side, with horse and carriage rides and moonlit strolls along the bayside seawall. And you won't want to miss nearby St. Augustine Lighthouse or the otherworldly colors and textures of the coquina rock beach at Washington Oaks Gardens.

Just across the state line, we felt right at home in the quaint coastal town of St. Marys, Georgia. The cute shops and old homes of the historic district brought us back to a time when this was a bustling seaport, and families sat drinking lemonade on their front porches to beat the heat.

As we strolled the streets of the historic district, we stopped to admire the state's second-oldest church, First Presbyterian, built in 1808. Then we visited nearby Oak Grove Cemetery, where Spanish moss drips from the live oaks that shade the fascinating stone grave markers of St. Marys' founders.

Egret at the St. Augustine Alligator Farm Zoological Park on Florida's Anastasia Island (right)

A rainbow of sea shells from the famed beaches of Sanibel Island on Florida's west coast (bottom)

We toured the Orange Hall and the National Seashore Museums, as well as the St. Marys Submarine Museum and Kings Bay Naval Base. Then we relaxed along the St. Marys River as commercial shrimp boats returned to port, casting mesmerizing reflections in the dark, glassy waters.

Unique celebrations include the Rock Shrimp Festival, the Crawfish Festival, the Catfish Festival and the Christmas White Lighting ceremony. St. Marys is also known as the gateway to Cumberland Island, where you can ferry over to see wild horses, undeveloped beaches and nature at its purest.

Our next stop brought us to South Carolina's legendary low country and a town named Beaufort. This Southern gem is the second-oldest city in South Carolina, and home to some of the first successful plantations in the New World. (They grew rice and indigo.)

South Carolina was the first state to secede from the Union, giving birth to the American Civil War. You can still witness evidence of the war's carnage at Sheldon Church. The skeletal remains of this once-beautiful brick building still lie in ruins after being burned in Gen. Sherman's march to the sea.

As shown in the movie *Forrest Gump*, Beaufort's Sea Islands

Looking back at our coastal journey, we were enriched by agriculture, history and a warm sense of community.

Rising moon at sunset in South Carolina's Hunting Island State Park

are its most treasured assets, offering endless fishing and shrimping opportunities.

St. Helena Island is home to a large community of Gullah people, whose African ancestors were brought to America to work on the rice plantations. Their customs blended with those of the white population, creating a new culture and language.

When the plantation owners imported the slaves, however, they also brought in malaria and yellow fever, which ran rampant in the hot, humid rice fields. These diseases drove the plantation owners away, leaving the Gullah culture to flourish through the generations.

South Carolina's beloved Hilton Head Island is its most popular vacation spot, offering shopping, restaurants and recreational beaches. Hunting Island, Parris Island and Fripp Island are just a few of the many beautiful places you'll find on the South Carolina coast.

Our last discovery of the southeastern coastal region was the town of Wilmington, North Carolina. We weren't surprised to find beautiful coastlines like Wrightsville Beach, where we fished from a graceful pier. But we were surprised at the historical and cultural depth of the area.

We toured the Burgwin-Wright Museum, which was Lord Cornwallis' last headquarters before the British Army surrendered to American troops in the Revolutionary War.

The *USS North Carolina*, a retired World War II battleship, serves as a floating memorial to the more than 10,000 North Carolina soldiers who have lost their lives in service to their country. The massive ship, which saw battle in the Pacific, survived a dangerous torpedo hit.

Another find in Wilmington was Screen Gems Studios, where more than 400 movies and television shows have been filmed. *Cape Fear*, *Firestarter*, *Matlock* and *Dawson's Creek* were all shot on location right here in town.

Looking back at our coastal journey, we were enriched by agriculture, history and a warm sense of community. The friendly people we met along the miles seemed to share one uniting sentiment: The salty breeze, warm sun and deep roots make the Southeast Coast an ideal place to visit or call home.

Becky and I will be forever grateful for the traffic jam on I-95. We discovered a wonderful region, and realized that even life's most trying moments can reveal peace and beauty. ✳

Sunlit moss on the coquina rock beach at Washington Oaks Gardens near St. Augustine, Florida

My Old Kentucky Home

A picturesque barn and paddocks in the Bluegrass region

The sun shines bright on the land of horses, rolling hills and Southern hospitality.

Story and photos by KENNY DUNN

From the elegant grace of the Bluegrass horse farms to the rugged beauty of the Appalachian foothills, eastern Kentucky offers up country splendor and charm that are second to none. Plus, the people are the most neighborly folks you'll likely find anywhere and are the epitome of hospitality.

Surely, this is God's Country.

I live in the tiny town of Bonnyman. You can't find it on most maps, but it's just up the road from Hazard in Perry County in the southeastern part of the state.

My Uncle Bill has owned a country store in Shuckybean Hollow in Bonnyman for 20 years, and before that, my grandfather and great-grandfather were the storekeepers for 40 years. I literally grew up there stocking shelves.

My relatives love to tell the story how as an infant, I cooled off on summer days, sitting in a washtub on the front porch of the store. I became as much a fixture of the place as the old Warm Morning stove.

Not much has changed there in 35 years since my washtub days. I still stop in almost every day.

The Red River Gorge in Powell County offers some of the most spectacular rock formations east of the Mississippi River. I'll always remember the time I took my mom there to see the sunrise over Auxier Ridge. The 360-degree views of the fog-shrouded valleys below the ridge are breathtaking.

The trail leading to that spot follows a forested path for almost 2 miles, before turning into a slender sandstone spine that is

Charming stone walls along a horse country back road

Sunset on an old barn and silo in Clark County

A well-worn saddle resting between rides

just a few feet wide, hundreds of feet high and drops straight down on both sides.

When Mom encountered this section of the trail, she looked out and saw how high up we were, then fell down on all fours and crawled back into the forest screaming. I'm sure glad no one was there to see—or hear—that!

Another of my favorite hiking trails is the Sheltowee Trace, which begins near Morehead and bisects the Daniel Boone National Forest for about 270 miles before ending at the Big South Fork National River Recreation Area on the Kentucky-Tennessee border.

My friend Steve, who shares my interest in photography, and I went hiking there one time in search of a waterfall at Pounders Branch. We followed a trail along the rim of a steep gorge, then bushwhacked through thick brush until we got to

59

Autumn colors at Eagle Falls in Cumberland Falls State Park

Crested dwarf irises, also known as blue flags

the stream. We had to wade upstream to finally get to the falls.

By the time we reached this isolated spot, we felt as though no one had ever been there before us. It offered a great sense of discovery that is hard to find nowadays.

The horse reigns supreme in the Bluegrass area around Lexington, and the farms that raise these magnificent creatures are simply splendid. I remember as a child visiting family in Lexington and driving through the beautiful countryside past these farms. The gently rolling hills gave my brother and me the feeling of weightlessness each time the car rolled over the crest of one of them.

One of the main highways out of my hometown is the Daniel Boone Parkway. After a long, barren winter, there is no more splendid sight than the redbuds and dogwoods that bloom along the roadway each spring. Every year at this time, I load up my family and take a trip to visit my grandmother's house in London. The profusion of color and contrast with winter inspire both the young and old.

Kenny's Uncle Bill's store in Shuckybean Hollow in the town of Bonnyman

A curious raccoon kit near its den in the woods

Haystack Rock in the Red River Gorge

Morning fog at Hensley Settlement, Cumberland Gap National Historical Park

The 360-degree views of the fog-shrouded valleys below the ridge are breathtaking.

Sunrise view from Cloudsplitter overlooking the Red River Gorge

Hay bales stacked for the winter beside a Jackson County barn

Redbuds in bloom in the Daniel Boone National Forest

I could talk all day about the great times I had growing up here in eastern Kentucky, and the many adventures I've had since then, but I know you have things you need to get back to.

However, I hope I've given you enough of a glimpse of our neck of the woods that you'll take time out from this busy world we live in and visit God's Country.

And if you ever get to Bonnyman, be sure to stop in at Uncle Bill's store in Shuckybean Hollow. You just might find Uncle Bill and me visiting on the bench out front. ✳

MIDWEST

Far from being flyover country, the Midwest offers a world of reasons to call this land home. Beauty blooms in the vast prairies, charming farms, rustic North Woods and sparkling Great Lakes.

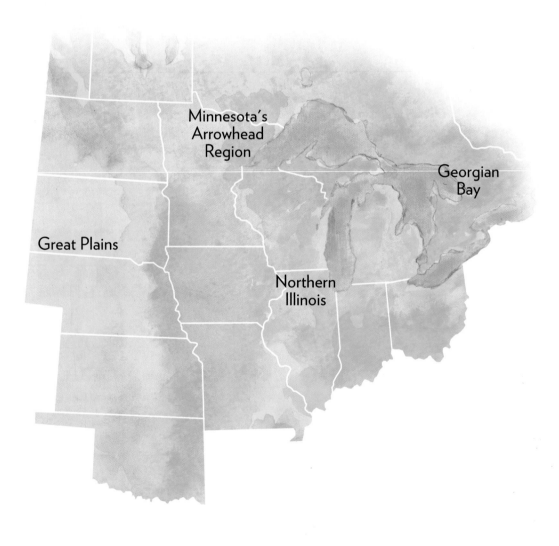

Minnesota's
Arrowhead
Region

Georgian
Bay

Great Plains

Northern
Illinois

Spectacular northern landscapes still lure modern-day explorers to Ontario's Georgian Bay.

Story and photos by MIKE GRANDMAISON

When my publisher asked me to take pictures of Georgian Bay for a new coffee-table book, I didn't hesitate for a second. Even here in Canada, surprisingly few people know much about this vast and beautiful body of water at the northeast end of Lake Huron. But I was born and raised a mere hour and a half from its northeastern shoreline, so Georgian Bay holds a special place in my heart.

Often called the sixth Great Lake, Georgian Bay is nearly as large as Lake Ontario, with more than 1,200 miles of scenic shoreline and 30,000 islands. On his first visit to the bay in 1615, French-Canadian explorer Samuel de Champlain originally named it *La Mer Douce* (The Sweetwater Sea).

The world's largest freshwater island, Manitoulin Island, forms the bay's northwestern shore, while Bruce Peninsula separates the bay from Lake Huron to the southwest.

The Canadian "Group of Seven" painters immortalized this part of the country with their bold, colorful and innovative approach to painting the landscape. Paintings such as *Stormy Weather, Georgian Bay* by Frederick Varley; *Island, Georgian Bay* by Franklin Carmichael; *A September Gale* and *Georgian Bay* by Arthur Lismer; and *Pine Island* by Tom Thomson capture the essence of this ruggedly picturesque corner of Ontario.

Artists of all genres continue this tradition today. I had the privilege of hiking and photographing in Killarney Provincial Park with local painting legend Jim Morlock.

Many scenic roads surround the bay, making exploration by

Land of Kitchikewana

Rough waters at Indian Head Cove in Bruce Peninsula National Park

One of Flowerpot Island's gravity-defying sea stacks

Legend of Kitchikewana

In the stories passed down from the Huron Indian tribe, a giant, ill-tempered god named Kitchikewana (kitch-ee-ka-WAH-nah) once protected Georgian Bay. He was so huge, it took thousands of bird feathers to make his headdress and 600 beaver pelts for his robe. He wore a necklace strung with tree stumps instead of beads.

One day, the other Huron gods decided Kitchikewana might be less cranky if they found him a girlfriend. So they gathered the most interesting girls from all the tribes in the region to meet him.

And sure enough, Kitchikewana fell in love with a beautiful maiden named Wanakita. The smitten god asked Wanakita if she wanted to be with him. But she was already in love with one of the warriors from her own tribe and turned him down.

In a fit of rage, Kitchikewana dug his fingers deep into the ground and threw great handfuls of dirt and rock into the water, creating the 30,000 islands. The five marks his fingers left in the ground became Midland Bay, Penetang Bay, Hog Bay, Sturgeon Bay and Matchedash Bay.

Heartbroken and exhausted, Kitchikewana lay down at the southern end of Georgian Bay and fell asleep, where he remains to this day. You can still see his gigantic form in the rocky, uninhabited island known as Giant's Tomb.

land fun and easy. To the east, Highways 69 and 400 lead from Sudbury to Barrie. A turn westward on Highway 26 from Barrie to Owen Sound follows the southern shoreline.

From Owen Sound, Highway 6 travels northward through the Bruce Peninsula to Tobermory, where you embark on the *M.S. Chi-Cheemaun* passenger and car ferry to South Baymouth on Manitoulin Island. There, Highway 6 continues north to Espanola. Another turn eastward on the Trans-Canada, or Highway 17, leads you back to Sudbury, the Nickel Capital of the World and my hometown.

Sitting in the heart of the Great Lakes-St. Lawrence Forest region, the bay features a lush forest landscape of red pine, eastern white pine and eastern hemlock, as well as hardwoods like yellow birch, red and sugar maple, and red and white oak.

In autumn, this is one of my favorite places to photograph fall colors, especially in the Killarney area. Whether it is backlit bright-orange sugar maple leaves against a crystal-clear sky,

or a close-up of a red maple leaf floating in a pool of cobalt blue water, opportunities abound.

Spring, summer and even winter offer their own pleasant opportunities for exploration and discovery on the bay. In spring, the fresh, green color of new foliage is a joy to behold.

I cherish winter mostly because it provides me with a quiet time for solitude. Photographically speaking, winter offers a "cleaner" landscape, since many of the distracting elements, like twigs and rocks, are covered with a deep blanket of snow.

Geologically speaking, a vast arc of granite bedrock known as the Canadian Shield runs through eastern Georgian Bay. This unforgiving rock formation—exposed during the last ice age—gives rise to some truly spectacular landscapes of windswept white pines and stony islands.

Western Georgian Bay, however, follows the mainly limestone Niagara Escarpment. It's along the Bruce Peninsula that Dr. Doug Larson discovered an ancient cliff-edge ecosystem

Dolomite rock in the clear waters of Bruce Peninsula National Park

Hardy pines grow from the time-worn rocks of French River Provincial Park

consisting of eastern white cedars, lichens and mosses growing on the ledges and inside the cracks of shoreline cliffs.

I also explored many secondary roads leading to a number of access points around the bay. They often included unbelievably beautiful areas where I could explore the landscape of a provincial or national park.

While I have had much success photographing Georgian Bay from the land, I've also explored it by water.

The easiest way to see the bay by water is to take a sightseeing trip on *The Island Queen*, Canada's largest sightseeing cruise ship. It originates from Parry Sound and explores the Thirty Thousand Island region of Georgian Bay, recently designated as a Biosphere Reserve by the United Nations.

During two- or three-hour cruises, you will enjoy some of this country's most spectacular coastline, from stunning glacier-sculpted islands of various colors to windswept, forested rocks as old as anything on this planet. You'll also spot some amazing cottages tucked into the rocky shoreline.

While the *M.S. Chi-Cheemaun* ferry cuts across the main channel and serves more as a transportation vessel, I nevertheless found opportunities to photograph the bay's vast expanses of open water from the ferry's decks.

On any given day, the waters of Georgian Bay can be as calm as a mirror or rough enough to make you seasick. Some days, you feel like you can see forever. Other days, the fog is so thick you can become disoriented just walking along the ship's deck!

To explore the bay on a more intimate level, I often used a motorboat, sailboat, canoe or kayak. I'm not fond of motors (I find them incongruous with the wilderness), but a motorboat provides a compromise between intimacy and speed.

Occasionally, I hired knowledgeable local guides to lead me to remote locations. I am convinced that I have actually walked onto at least a few islands that no one else has ever stepped on before! Even if mine weren't the first footsteps, though, I felt a wonderful sense of adventure on each island I explored.

Canoes and kayaks offer an even more intimate connection

Maple leaves, pinecones and bunchberry plants near Tyson Lake

A cute red fox kit outside his den along the bay's north shore

Flowerpot Island light station at Fathom Five National Marine Park

White pines and rocky islands at the end of the Chikanishing Trail

as you skim over the surface of the bay, barely an inch or two from the water. It's absolutely wonderful in calm, glasslike conditions. But to a novice kayaker like me, the bay can be quite overwhelming when the waters get rough.

It's difficult to describe the feeling of freedom and solitude you get from gliding from one island to another, then stepping onto the shore to take photos, rest on the sun-baked granite or cool off in the clear, aqua-colored waters. Those who have experienced this pleasure rarely forget it.

Taking photographs while paddling a canoe or kayak does require protection for your equipment, both from splashing during rough waters or, heaven forbid, from capsizing! I keep my photo equipment tucked inside waterproof containers.

My travels took me through a variety of public parks along the shores of Georgian Bay, including three national and eight provincial parks.

Bruce Peninsula National Park on the Niagara Escarpment is one of the largest protected areas in southern Ontario. The famous Bruce Trail starts at Tobermory and offers hikers some 500 miles of trails, ending at Queenston in southern Ontario. This park provides habitat for an abundance of orchid species as well as the rare lakeside daisy and the dwarf lake iris. Georgian Bay Islands National Park includes Beausoleil Island, important habitat for the threatened eastern massasauga rattlesnake.

You'll find an interesting collection of lighthouses and shipwrecks in Fathom Five National Marine Park. Accessible

A lovely day for canoeing in Killarney Provincial Park

only by boat, the park also includes famously picturesque Flowerpot Island's two limestone sea stacks (a third fell down in 1903). I was able to photograph a couple of the shipwrecks from the small tour boat that took me to Flowerpot Island.

Of the provincial parks, Killarney, on the east side of the bay, is the crown jewel of the Ontario Parks system, renowned for clear, sapphire blue lakes and rewarding hiking trails.

It also features one of the oldest mountain ranges in the world. According to geologists, the La Cloche Mountains—made of ancient white quartzite rock—were originally taller than the Rocky Mountains! I explored the hills on the north shore of Killarney Lake. After scrambling to the top, I was rewarded with breathtaking vistas of water, rock and trees.

French River Provincial Park is remote and accessible only by water, but offers spectacular views of tree-lined shores. My friends Estelle and Rick Lapointe were kind enough to guide me through this remote area, which Rick knows from his youth.

The southern section of Georgian Bay flattens out into a heavily populated shoreline that's just 90 minutes from Toronto. Residents and visitors alike enjoy many of the fine white sand beaches, including Wasaga Beach. At nearly 9 miles, it's the longest freshwater beach in the world.

The Georgian Bay area offers an incredibly rich and diverse landscape to explore. A trip to this fascinating area will certainly reward you with wonderful memories and perhaps even a few photographic gems. Georgian Bay is, after all, God's Country! ✷

A *Sense* of
Stewardship

Cheerful red farm buildings along a rural road in Ogle County

In Northern Illinois, there's something worth preserving around every bend of the road.

Story and photos by TERRY DONNELLY

It's a summer evening and I'm driving due north on a narrow gravel road with the sun low on the horizon. Over my right shoulder I'm being paced by the lengthening shadow of my vehicle rippling over the perfect rows of soybeans extending to the east. This place is flat.

Like all country roads in Northern Illinois, this one has a number and surely a name, although I know neither. I spotted a wind farm from Interstate Highway 39 just north of Mendota and took the first available turnoff. Initially it was a blacktop, complete with center lines and a groomed shoulder. Then it turned into a narrow unlined blacktop with a nicely mowed shoulder. Finally it became this unpaved but solid gravel road, again with well-tended margins. I am thrilled to explore the local countryside in this spectacular evening light.

Although I live in the Pacific Northwest, I was born in LaSalle County in Northern Illinois and spent 40 years getting to know this country and its seasons. "Aimless" driving in evening light like this reminds me of my early days as a professional photographer. Agricultural magazines were my first paying clients; they had a monthly appetite for cover images of beautiful farms like the ones that surrounded me.

Nearly a quarter-century later, my visits are filled with both nostalgia and the anticipation of discovering changes. New wind farms are probably the most dramatic change to the landscape; rising above the level fields and farms, they are visible for miles. With the consistent wind patterns in the

My visits are filled with both
nostalgia and the **anticipation**
of discovering changes.

Blue vervain (left) on rolling prairie grassland in Nachusa Grasslands Conservation Area

Sunflowers (below) in Lee County's Green River State Wildlife Area

Red Covered Bridge, built in 1863 over Big Bureau Creek (opposite) near Princeton

north-central part of the state, Illinois is now ranked fourth in the nation for wind power capacity.

Some consider wind farms eyesores, but I don't mind seeing them. To my eye, the juxtaposition of an ancient weathered barn in front of a gleaming white wind turbine against a blue sky works well. Both reflect our evolving technology. A row of windowpanes above a large barn door hints that the structure may predate electricity. Now these wind farms are taking their turn illuminating our lives—literally.

In this warm light, it's the condition of the roadside ditches and shoulders that elicits the greatest nostalgia. They are mostly mowed, tended and trim; they look like lawns. Farmers in these parts keep things neatly groomed and commonly mow all the way from the house right up to the edge of the county road. I used to take the well-tended, tidy aesthetics for granted. After years of travel, I now recognize it as exceptional.

Of course all this lawn care reflects a community attitude of pride and involvement—a sense of stewardship that continues to evolve. Owners with a newfound interest in conservation and habitat restoration have converted many roadside strips and vacant fields and pastures to native prairie grasses.

Still, it is no secret that the predominant landscape here is agricultural. Vast fields of soybeans and corn cover the flat to

Wind turbines towering over a cornfield on the Crescent Ridge wind farm

Matthiessen Falls from the Upper Dells in Matthiessen State Park

A Putnam County farm embraced by cornfields and wooded hills

Corn harvest in Bureau County

Hardwood forest in fall color on the west rim of Illinois Canyon

Autumn color along Ottawa Canyon in Starved Rock State Park

Snow on Armstrong Creek in Starved Rock State Park

gently rolling land. Illinois typically ranks second nationally in corn and soybean production, and fourth in hog production.

Exploring country roads in these parts can be a real pleasure. Even nondescript gravel lanes have considerable historic significance. Without them, farmers didn't have access to fields, and grains didn't go to market.

They're mostly laid out on a grid, making it nearly impossible to get lost. Drive any direction long enough and you eventually come to a county "hard" road or state road. Even if it takes you a little out of your way, it's bound to lead you through some very interesting small towns and hamlets—places like Prairie Center, Tiskilwa, West Brooklyn, Buda, Scales Mound, Bishop Hill and Grand Detour. These places may not seem like much of a destination, but they all offer something special. Even if it's little more than a crossroads or an isolated economic center, each hamlet is like a museum filled with rural architecture.

As much as I artistically appreciate man's imprint on the landscape, I also have a photographic enthusiasm for the natural environment. In this part of the country, that means the tallgrass prairie.

Although the native prairie has been largely displaced by agriculture and urban development, many remnants can still be found around the state. Rare scraps of virgin prairie in pioneer cemeteries and along railroad easements are now augmented with acres of prairie restoration in formerly fallow fields, roadsides and private gardens.

Prairies also are found in locations where St. Peter sandstone sits just beneath the earth's surface. This rock resisted plowing,

The Mississippi River from the bluffs of Mississippi Palisades State Park

A heavy dusting of snow on a farmstead in LaSalle County

and preserved the prairie grass above. Two notable remnants of the unplowed prairie are Nachusa Grasslands, a Nature Conservancy preserve of 3,100 acres near Franklin Grove, and Goose Lake Prairie State Natural Area, with about 2,500 acres preserved as a state park near Morris.

These prairies put on their finest show in late summer with cord grass and big bluestem rising several feet among blossoms of coneflowers, black-eyed Susans, goldenrod and bee balm.

Although Illinois' sandstone resisted the plow, it gave way to erosion in a spectacular fashion, most dramatically at Starved Rock and Matthiessen State Parks. These are among the crown jewels of Illinois' natural areas.

Located along the Illinois River Valley in LaSalle County, where numerous streams and creeks have eroded the ubiquitous sandstone, the parks contain deep, sculpted and colorful canyons amid deciduous hardwood forests.

Hiking these canyons is an escape to another world. They are cool and shaded in the summer and sheltered from the elements on the windiest of winter days.

In spring, a trail in almost any of the parks' canyons will wind along small streams, pools and waterfalls decorated with carpets of bluebells and other wildflowers.

The most amazing seasonal attraction is the autumn show of colors in the hardwood forest, which is intensified by the orange hues of the canyon's sandstone walls.

These canyons and prairies and farmlands gave me my start, both in life and in my profession. This landscape shows us our history, our innovations, our limitations and our place; its vastness creates space for introspection and wonder.

I carry these Northern Illinois landscapes with me, and it is my privilege to be able to share them with others who are curious about what we can find along the road. ✳

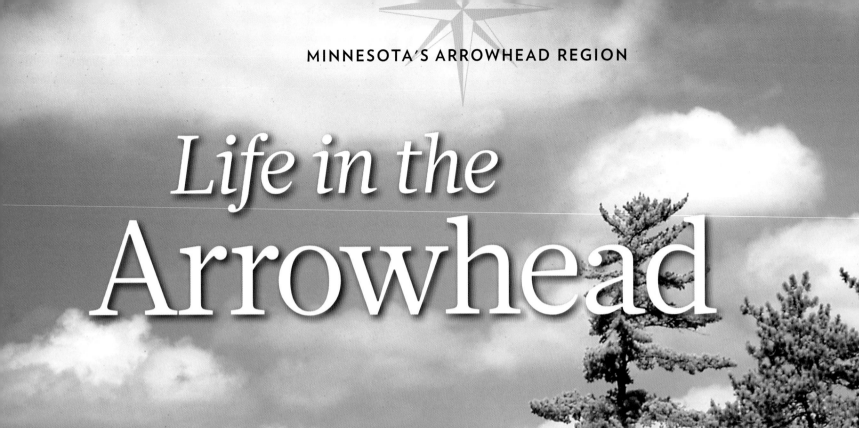

Life in the Arrowhead

Rustic cabin on Burntside Lake in Boundary Waters Canoe Area Wilderness

Explore the wonders of this North Woods gem set in the crystal waters of Lake Superior.

Story and Photos by BOB FIRTH

It's like the pull on a compass needle that just naturally points me "up north" to Minnesota's scenic Arrowhead Region. I live in the Twin Cities and have made the journey many times over the past 50 years. Yet every time I can't wait to strap a canoe on my car, pack my camera gear and head back there again.

This section of far northeastern Minnesota is so named because it looks like an arrowhead jutting eastward to Lake Superior. But like me, you'll also call it God's Country once you experience its countless lakes, cascading rivers, seemingly endless forests and other hidden treasures.

On the western end of the Arrowhead Region is Itasca State Park, where the Mississippi River begins. Believe it or not, at the headwaters of this mighty river, you can actually tiptoe across on stepping-stones from one shore to the other. My family has done it many times—sometimes gracefully and other times with a big splash.

This part of Minnesota also brings back fond childhood memories of wild ricing. When I was high school age, I used to make the four-hour drive north in the late summer with a group of buddies to harvest wild rice that thrives in the cold waters of the lakes and streams.

We made good money, and we'd take our earnings and camp and fish for a week or so. It was a time blessed with wholesome life lessons mixed with good old-fashioned fun.

Interestingly enough, I found myself back again 30 years

Sunrise in Superior National Forest

later—this time as a professional photographer hired to document Native Americans harvesting wild rice as they have for centuries, in a boat propelled by a duck pole through the clear, shallow waters. It was a wonderful experience, except for the part where our boat nearly tipped over and tossed me into the water, camera and all.

Heading east, one of my favorite stops is the tiny town of Embarrass. Notorious for often being the coldest spot in the nation, it's also a mighty cool place to visit. I'm not sure how the settlement got its name, but it certainly has nothing to be embarrassed about.

This area is best known as iron ore country, where taconite

is mined. It is, beyond that, amazingly beautiful country with Midwestern mountains draped with forests of all kinds. It's also dotted with crystal-clear, sky-blue lakes that look like jewels set in a tapestry of velvet-green trees and reddish-brown rock. And I love to study the craftsmanship of the town's historic log buildings built by Finnish settlers.

My fascination with historic log structures also guided me to a beautifully wooded area not far from Ely, where the narrow, winding road leads to the Great Lakes School of Log Building, which was established in 1975 by master log builder and instructor Ron Brodigan.

Ron is a lumberjack, inexhaustible conversationalist and a

Roaring High Falls of the Pigeon River on the Minnesota-Canada border

Native Americans' wild rice harvest

highly intellectual jack-of-all-trades. More than that, he's a genuine North Woods icon, an American gem in the rough, in whose aura and presence I was awed.

My time there was topped off by a lantern-light moose dinner prepared to perfection by Ron. The accommodations for the students and me were various log cabins built by former students, where I read by lantern light with my dog by my side, listening to wolves howl in the forest and the wind whispering through the trees.

The Boundary Waters Canoe Area Wilderness is a maze of endless lakes, islands, rivers, portages and trails. You could spend years of vacation time paddling this expansive wilderness and never visit the same place twice.

When I'm of a mind to use a motor on a boat instead of a paddle, I go to Voyageurs National Park. This Minnesota and Canadian wilderness is a labyrinth of monster lakes and islands. The fishing there is tremendous.

Once, instead of tent camping, we rented a houseboat and shared the experience with my father. What an adventure that was in the land where trappers, voyageurs (professional canoemen who hauled furs) and lumberjacks once roamed.

The eastern side of the Arrowhead Region brings me to my favorite spot: the North Shore. Many people think that everything north of Lake Superior is in Canada, but Minnesota has a 153-mile-long "trail" running northeast along the shoreline from Duluth to the Canadian border. Even though it's really Highway 61, I call it a trail because it makes me feel like I've gone back in time to the days of the early explorers.

A sparkling Boundary Waters lake from the Gunflint Trail

The spectacular mating dance of a loon

My friend "Captain" Terry Heim during a photography trip on Gunflint Lake

My family loves to walk the shoreline
in search of driftwood, agates and other treasures.

Lighthouse atop the cliffs at Split Rock State Park

The Temperance River in Temperance State Park

Brilliant fall foliage in Superior National Forest

As often as I have set out to "discover" the North Shore, I have always found something new and unexpected along the road, in the birch forests or on the miles and miles of inviting rivers, streams and hiking trails.

The first maps of the region date back to the 1600s, when French explorers canoed and hiked here. And the land still retains its primitive essence today. Lake Superior is the world's largest freshwater lake in terms of surface area and one of the most dangerous bodies of water in the world. Sudden violent storms have wrecked hundreds of ships through the centuries.

Looking across such a vast lake from the dramatic shoreline it has carved from solid rock, I am filled with respect for Mother Nature's raw power. That power is equally evident—and beautiful—in the fast-moving rivers with hundreds of spectacular waterfalls that plummet toward the lake.

My family loves to walk the shoreline in search of driftwood, agates and other treasures that this magnificent lake may have washed ashore. The boys especially enjoy challenging each other to see who can tolerate the cold water longest—quite a test of wills, since there is often ice on the lake well into May.

On calm days, I have taken my canoe or kayak out on the lake to photograph a different perspective of the shoreline, but always with a watchful eye for Lake Superior's legendary and unpredictable storms. I'm awestruck as I witness these approaching storms and watch the waves grow in height and strength as they crash to the shore.

It's all part of the magnetic pull that keeps me going up north to God's Country again and again. ✳

A Kind of Hardscrabble
Splendor

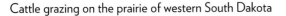

Cattle grazing on the prairie of western South Dakota

The beauty of the Great Plains runs through its vast landscapes and the strength of its people.

Story and photos by GREG LATZA

I come from a long line of South Dakota farmers, and I'm proud of that fact. While my tool is now a camera instead of a tractor, it wasn't always that way.

I spent my youth toiling alongside my father in the fields and pastures of our Sanborn County farm. I was driving a pickup by age 9 and combining oats at 11. I was trusted with everything except planting corn, which Dad reserved for himself. He was notorious for having painstakingly straight rows, and I wasn't about to mess with perfection.

There were countless late winter nights when I was called out of my warm bed to help pull a backward calf, and Saturday mornings were reserved for cleaning out the hog barns. My teenage muscles were toned from throwing bales, stretching fences and doing nearly every form of work you can think of that occurs on a Midwestern farm.

When I was about halfway through college at South Dakota State University, the time came to decide if the farm was my future. I decided it was not. My sister and her husband were eager to take over, and I was happy for them. Photography had wrestled my heart away from the daily grind of farming.

But your heart never really leaves farming. There's a famous saying that goes, "You can take the boy off the farm, but you can't take the farm out of the boy." Those words could not ring more true for me.

As I see it, I now have the best of both worlds. My photography has always had strong ties to the land. As a result, I spend much

Harvesting wheat in Montana

A future South Dakota farmer in the driver's seat

A display of heartfelt Americana in Nebraska

of my time traveling through and photographing farm and ranch country, and I also get to meet many of the great people across the Great Plains.

There is a general sameness to these people. That's not to say that they are plain or dull—quite the opposite is true. Rather, they are made of the same cloth because they've had the same general experiences.

Most of these folks are modest and hardworking and possess a special confidence gained when you live and earn a living on the land. And they have a generally mischievous nature and an ability to use humor to deal with the daily realities of surviving on the Plains.

It's my belief that only a certain type of person can live on the Great Plains, and that the characteristics of these people have been carried down through the generations all the way back from the homesteaders. A strong will is required to live in a sod house on the barren Plains. And how can a person spend

days or weeks on end scratching the same patch of dry ground with a one-bottom plow, using both mind and muscle to do so, if he or she isn't as stubborn as the mule pulling that plow? To deal with all of the curveballs thrown at them during every day of their existence, the homesteaders surely used humor. Wrapped around all these hardscrabble qualities was a strong faith in both God and their family to help get them through life.

Those very same characteristics—strong-willed, stubborn, faithful and humorous—accurately describe the folks who live on the Great Plains today. They are a noble bunch, and they know they live in a special place—maybe one of the last great places on Earth.

The famous explorers Lewis and Clark repeatedly wrote about the grandeur of the Great Plains as they first crossed this region in 1804. They described vast herds of bison grazing on endless horizons of grass, and documented dozens of plants and animals then unknown to man. It was a bonanza of new

Hardy bison during a South Dakota winter

Formerly the Saline County Bank, on National Register of Historic Places

A time-worn church in western North Dakota

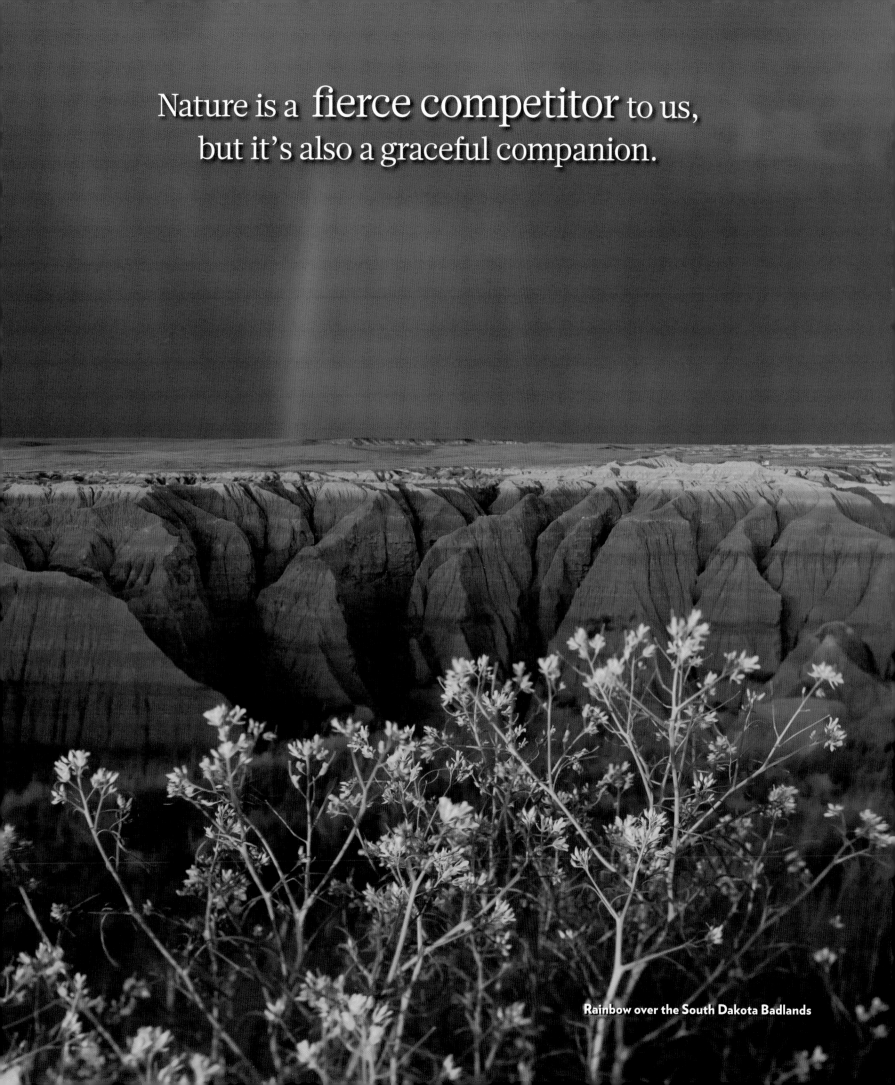

Nature is a **fierce competitor** to us, but it's also a graceful companion.

Rainbow over the South Dakota Badlands

Friday night football in Flandreau, South Dakota (left)

Sunset conversation on a Great Plains farm in Oklahoma (below)

A young dancer at a powwow in Lower Brule, South Dakota (opposite)

information about a land that no one knew about, except for the American Indians who had been living with the glories and hardships of Great Plains life for centuries.

Today's Great Plains residents have much in common with those Native Americans. We tolerate the travelers who pass through and chuckle amongst ourselves at some of the odd things they say. One of the more common utterances by tourists and Southern business travelers is "How can you live in such a cold place?" Well, we just do, I guess.

How can someone from the Great Plains explain the splendid and drastic change of seasons to someone who doesn't live it? Seasons are like a narcotic to most of us; we experience one and look forward to the next—except winter. That's another story.

Gradually easing out of winter, we yearn for the ice to melt and for the snow to yield the first green shoots of spring. It's a time of rebirth on the Plains, and it's made that much more special because of the lifeless deep freeze we've left behind. New calves and ewes soak up the warm sun, and pastures take on emerald hues we haven't seen for months.

All too soon for some, this magical time gives way to summer. Lots of people around the country don't realize it gets hot here,

Cattle roundup on a South Dakota ranch

too. Triple-digit temperatures aren't that uncommon in the heart of July and August. But with the heat comes a time of celebration for hundreds of small towns across the Plains; street dances mix with school reunions and centennial parades. It's a fine excuse to loosen up for just a little while. There's still plenty of work, but it's not quite as urgent as in spring and definitely not as pressing as the following season's tasks.

For me, autumn is the best season. A lifelong hunter, I enjoy nothing more than to use the excuse to get outside and breathe crisp air and view the changing colors. On the farm, there was a delicate balance between harvest and hunting. If it was too wet to combine corn, then it was probably an ideal morning for duck hunting.

Even winter has its charm, at least for a few weeks. Foggy December nights flock every tree, fence post and blade of grass with wondrous frost, and such glorious morning sights were some of my first inspirations to grab a camera. Christmas on the farm is a special time as well.

But January marks the beginning of the roughest part of Plains living. Subzero temperatures for days on end, howling blizzards and drifted roads all make spring that much more desirable when the cycle begins again.

But even in that most rugged of weather, there is a sense of accomplishment. A satisfaction comes from knowing that we are surviving—maybe even thriving—in some of the country's harshest conditions. The early Plains settlers must have felt that

A flock of sandhill cranes on their migration through Nebraska

way when they emerged from their sod houses and saw that they had conquered the prairie winter and that the temperature would soon be rising again.

The upper Great Plains are often labeled "flyover states" by those who haven't actually taken the time to stop. Anyone who casually considers us worthy of only flying over is obviously ignorant of the natural beauty that we enjoy every day.

It's everywhere you look, whether on a bright green spring afternoon or in the reds and golds of an autumn evening on the prairie. It's even there on the coldest of January mornings, if you take the time to look at the intricate patterns of drifting snow or maybe the rainbowlike sun dogs bookending the sun on an especially frigid morning.

Nature is a fierce competitor to us, but it's also a graceful companion to those who stop long enough to appreciate it. The beauty is not only all around us, but it's also inside of us—not only in the landscape but also in its people.

That's why it's so comforting to live here. Neighbors show their inner beauty by banding together to do someone's chores when they are sick or even to stage an entire harvest for a family that lost a loved one. The gestures can also be small— just a simple "finger wave" from atop the steering wheel, the laughter around the local coffee shop table, and in a simple offering of free sweet corn if you come and pick it yourself.

Who wouldn't want to live here on the Great Plains? It's truly God's Country. ✳

WEST

Hardy pioneers forged westward to search for wide open spaces and explore the great unknown. Many stayed to put down roots, but this land is still wild, spacious and spectacular.

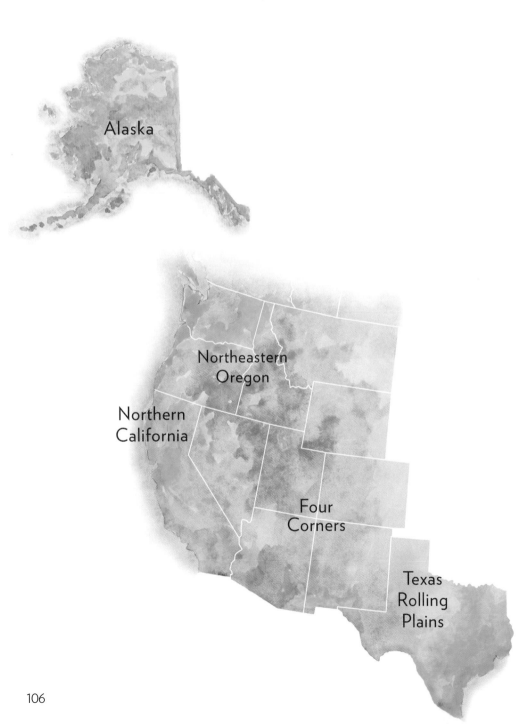

Alaska

Northeastern Oregon

Northern California

Four Corners

Texas Rolling Plains

He's home on the range in Texas' Rolling Plains.

Story and photos by RUSSELL GRAVES

I moved to the Texas Rolling Plains back in the summer of 1993. I'd never been that far west in Texas, but relished the opportunity for a new adventure. Fresh out of college with a new degree, new job and new wife, I felt like a pioneer striking out across the West to stake a claim on a new life. I grew up in northeast Texas and was unaccustomed to such wide-open spaces and elbow room.

Situated in the upper midsection of Texas, the Rolling Plains begin west of Fort Worth and cut a wide swath through rolling red-dirt hills all the way into the Panhandle. The Caprock Escarpment marks the dividing line between the Rolling Hills and High Plains. It rises abruptly from the plains to heights of nearly 1,000 feet in some spots. Along the boundary, erosion has carved deep badlands like Palo Duro Canyon, Blanco Canyon and breaks along the Canadian River, which are especially dramatic when you consider how dry this part of Texas is.

Within a week of moving to Childress, I found myself standing along the edge of the Pease River. The Pease is a usually dry river that flows with a shallow trickle of water through the heart of the Rolling Plains during the winter. The rest of the year, the only time you'll see water is after an angry thunderstorm unleashes its fury in the form of lightning, high winds, hail, buckets of rain and an occasional tornado.

That day was a bit misty and a light fog shrouded the badlands. Droplets of water kissed my checks and a slight breeze gave me a chill, even though it was late summer. I sat on a ledge and

Stronghold of Cowboys & Cotton

There's work to be done, but not before a little fishing

The rugged Caprock Escarpment near Quitaque

The Panhandle town where the father of country swing music got his start

looked out across the river. I noticed how the junipers emitted a sweet, musky odor and swayed rhythmically in the breeze. I could hear cattle lowing down in the river bottom, although the thick salt cedars hid their exact location. Rolling Plains satisfy all the senses: sight, sound, smell, touch and even the taste of the fragrance in the air.

As I watched wild pigs scramble across the river, I marveled at how unyielding this land is against the forces of time and history. The Rolling Plains were one of the last areas of Texas to be settled, and because of that, all of the towns are barely a century old.

Before the settlers came, the region was home to as many as 10 million bison and nomadic tribes of Comanche Indians that depended on the bison for food, clothing and shelter.

In the Reconstruction era after the Civil War, the nation was expanding and hungered for beef. Vast stretches of grasslands that once fed the bison gave rise to some of the nation's largest and most historic cattle ranches. At one point the Burnett family's Four Sixes Ranch covered nearly a third of a million acres. The Four Sixes, along with many other historic ranches, still thrive in the Rolling Plains. They have colorful names like the Tongue River Ranch, Pitchfork and Triangle, and they continue to supply our nation and the world with beef.

The ranches also provide another benefit: They help keep the cowboy culture alive. On many of the Rolling Plains ranches, cowboys still gather and work cattle on horseback. Much of the ranch country is rough, and the only way to round up cattle is by a skilled cowboy on a steady horse.

Working cattle on horseback

Center pivot irrigation rig in a thirsty cotton field

Much of the ranch country is rough, and the only way to round up cattle is by a **skilled cowboy** on a steady horse.

Salt Creek, a spring-fed tributary of the fabled Red River

Artistic, soil-conserving patterns of terraced farm fields

Back at the pens, you'll still find cowboys roping calves near the branding fire, while a chuck wagon cook prepares dinner under a fly tent—much as they did more than 100 years ago. Sometimes you'll hear folks say the cowboy is a dying breed. I'll bet they've never been to this part of Texas.

Where cattle don't graze, farmers till the land and grow a variety of crops, including wheat, peanuts and hay. But cotton is king in the Texas Rolling Plains. Each fall, thousands of acres of farmland turn white with the big bolls of a healthy crop.

Texas grows about half the cotton produced in the U.S., and the Rolling Plains account for about 20 percent of that.

The area's farms and ranches provide ideal habitat for a variety of wildlife. Big species like wild pigs, white-tailed and mule deer roam the plains, while underfoot you'll find Texas horned lizards, wild turkeys, prairie dogs and coyotes. There are mountain lions and bobcats around here, too.

Mesquite trees, yucca and prickly pear cactus thrive on the rangeland. Along drainages, you'll find big cottonwood trees,

Like Nowhere Else on Earth

New Mexico's Shiprock, revered in Navajo legend as the Rock with Wings

In the midst of all this desolate beauty,
snow-fed rivers nurture unexpected life.

Navajo-tended sheep near Sentinel Mesa in Arizona's Monument Valley

Lightning over New Mexico's remote Bisti/De-Na-Zin Wilderness

Fanciful rock formations on Baby Rocks Mesa near Kayenta, Arizona

live on the reservation, which covers 27,000 square miles. That's an area larger than 10 of our 50 states.

Most of the land is used to raise sheep, a way of life the Navajo learned from Spanish conquistadors who settled the Four Corners in the mid-1500s. Just as they did then, many Navajo still live in traditional earthen hogans, with doors that always face east to catch the morning sun and good blessings.

The fourth corner, in southwest Colorado, is on the Ute Mountain Indian Reservation. The Utes in Colorado live on two separate, side-by-side reservations and are mainly engaged in raising cattle.

Guests are welcome at the many tribal events, but the most spectacular are the Gathering of Nations Powwow in Albuquerque in April, and the Intertribal Indian Ceremony at Red Rock State Park in Gallup, New Mexico, in August. I highly recommend both.

This area was also the center of the ancient Anasazi culture, which flourished for 1,000 years before they abandoned their hauntingly beautiful cliff dwellings around 1200 A.D. Some of the finest examples remain in remarkably good shape in Colorado's Mesa Verde National Park, west of Durango.

If you head north from Durango toward Ouray on the Million Dollar Highway, you'll find some of the best mountain scenery in the West. The highway's name comes from the million-dollar views to be had from Highway 550. With more than 100 peaks over 13,000 feet and 14 of Colorado's 14,000-foot peaks, it isn't false advertising.

In addition to tremendous mountain and alpine scenery, you'll find two of the most famous wildflower locations in the West: Yankee Boy Basin, which is west of Ouray, and my favorite, Ice Basin, west of Silverton. Ice Basin remains relatively undiscovered.

In addition to sightseeing, you can try your hand at fly-fishing on the Dolores River, white-water rafting the Animas

Pond on Molas Pass in the San Juan Mountains of Colorado

and hang gliding in Telluride.

If you enjoy hiking and four-wheeling, there are more than 500 miles of dirt roads in this part of the San Juan Mountains. Built in the 1800s as stagecoach or mining supply routes, these rugged roads offer views that will dazzle your soul and steal what breath you have left at this altitude.

The Colorado corner has culture, too, such as Telluride's bluegrass and film festivals and distinctive art galleries in Ouray and Silverton. But the Four Corners area still leans far more toward rustic than refined.

For really great fall color, plan on the last week of September through the first week of October. In a good year, the fall color in southwest Colorado will rival the best fall color anywhere in the United States. My favorite areas for leaf peeping are the Dallas Divide, Mount Sneffels, Owl Creek Pass and mountains around Silver Jack Reservoir.

Mount Sneffels and a long ridge of ragged peaks form one of Colorado's most scenic mountain escarpments and a must-visit location. Spring in the high altitudes—where you find the Colorado state flower, the columbine—doesn't arrive until early July.

Heading west into southeast Utah brings you into its famed red rock formations and miles of broad, rolling sandstone dunes known as "slick rock."

This colorful terrain is the stuff of mountain bikers' dreams, contributing to Utah's reputation as the bicycling capital of the world. The area is equally beloved for its excellent boating, horseback riding (an excellent way to see Monument Valley), scenic driving and river running.

The Navajo Nation's most scenic tribal park, Monument Valley, starts here, and is often called the eighth wonder of the world. After you see it, I think you will agree.

Add in Mexican Hat, The Goosenecks State Park, Valley of the Gods, Natural Bridges National Monument, Canyonlands National Park and the northeast part of Lake Powell, and you have another scenic blockbuster.

The state claims "The Greatest Snow on Earth," but many call it "The Greatest Show on Earth." It lives up to both titles as far as I'm concerned.

Utah's corner is particularly appealing toward the end of the monsoon season, in late August. That's when two months of

Crystal Lake off the Million Dollar Highway south of Ouray, Colorado

summer rain have greened up everything and toned down the temperatures. Crisp, clear air, dramatic clouds and rainbows are the norm. Some years, you'll get a second wildflower bloom in late August through September.

If magnificent solitude appeals to you, try visiting Monument Valley in winter. I was there several years ago right after a rare and beautiful January snowstorm. I shared the park with a grand total of five other visitors, which is amazing for a place this famous.

When you're looking for spring flowers, like the beautiful desert primrose, May's your month, but only in years when winter and spring are wet.

Driving south into Arizona, you get into the heart of Monument Valley, or *Tse' Bii Ndzisgaii*, as the Navajo call it. In the 1930s, director John Ford saw photos of Monument Valley taken by famed photographer Joseph Muench, and decided to film the movie *Stagecoach* here. The rest, as they say, is history.

Since then, hundreds of films, television shows and magazines have used Monument Valley as a backdrop. The view from the visitor's center is a scene of extraordinary beauty, with the landmark buttes of West Mitten, East Mitten and Merrick soaring above the valley.

The 17-mile self-drive loop road will take you right into the middle of the Monuments, past some truly unforgettable

Traditional earthen hogans, still home to many Navajo families

Native American petroglyphs at Utah's Newspaper Rock Historic Monument

Cliff Palace, ruins of an Anasazi Indian village, in Colorado's Mesa Verde National Park

Green River Overlook in Utah's Canyonlands National Park

Animas River on the Southern Ute Indian Reservation in Colorado

scenery. Other scenic gems I visit whenever I can include Little Monument Valley in the Round Rock Area, White Mesa Bridge, Window Rock and Canyon De Chelly National Monument.

Northwestern New Mexico is perhaps the most diverse of all the four corners. It ranges from flat, fertile irrigated farmland on the Navajo Agriculture Products Industry's vast acreage to massive, otherworldly rock formations. Shiprock, the towering basalt core of an extinct volcano, is known as *Tse bida hi*, or Rock with Wings, to the Navajo. In their legends, it was the ship that brought their ancestors to this land.

The distinct Western American cowboy culture first took root here in New Mexico, leaving a rich tradition of ranching in the area. You'll also find Angel Peak Recreation Area, Aztec National Monument, Chaco Canyon National Park and Red Rock State Monument. Legend, tradition and beauty combine to make this quadrant of the Four Corners "The Land of Enchantment."

Since the altitude and plant life in New Mexico are similar to that in Arizona and Utah, the best times to visit are similar also. But add a window in mid-October, when you'll find good cottonwood fall color in the Farmington and Aztec areas.

If I had to rank all of the things I love most about the Four Corners, I'd put its tremendous diversity of landscapes at the top of my list. Add endless country roads and a thriving rural lifestyle, and you truly have a place like no place else on Earth.

So bring your camera, your curiosity and an open mind, and you'll find a lifetime of unforgettable memories here in our four corners of God's Country. ✶

The Wonders of
Wallowa

The OK Quarter Circle Ranch near Joseph

They found heaven on Earth
in this rugged corner of Oregon.

Story and photos by DAVID JENSEN

The Cascade Mountains run north to south through Oregon and split the state into two distinct regions. The west is lush with vegetation, thanks to frequent rains from storms that blow in off the Pacific Ocean.

The Cascades block many of these weather systems, creating a "rain shadow" and a more arid climate in the eastern two-thirds of the state. I grew up on the wet side of the mountains, which has its own unique beauty. But about 30 years ago, I moved to the dry side of the Cascades to enjoy the invigorating, sunny weather and spectacular scenery.

My wife, Cathy, and I now make our home in the small town of Enterprise in the state's remote northeast corner. She's a city girl from Melbourne, Australia, but wholeheartedly agrees that this is God's Country.

We live at the edge of the Eagle Cap Wilderness Area, which is part of the Wallowa Mountains. At 358,541 acres, it's the largest designated wilderness in Oregon. With several peaks of nearly 10,000 feet, Wallowa County contains more above-timberline acreage than any other place in the state.

During the last ice age, these mountains were mantled by a 330-square-mile system of glaciers. The glaciers are mostly gone now, but they left behind all the classic landforms of alpine country: U-shaped valleys, cirques, moraines, tarns, cols and sharp peaks.

Not far away to the east, the earth appears to open up into an abyss called Hells Canyon. I suppose it's somewhat ironic to

Nez Perce commemorative dance at Chief Joseph Days

have a place with such a name in God's Country. But it's typical of the contrasts you'll find in this rugged corner of Oregon.

Hells Canyon is the deepest river gorge in North America. Carved by the Snake River, it plunges more than a mile below Oregon's west rim and 8,000 feet below He Devil Peak in the Seven Devils Mountains on the Idaho side. There are 900 miles of trails in the Hells Canyon National Recreation Area. I've hiked about 200 of those miles, so I've got a lot of beautiful country left to explore.

One of the virtues of living in such a rugged land is the option for quick climate control. Within the space of a few miles, you can change the weather—and even the season of the year—simply by seeking out a higher or lower elevation. The native Nez Perce tribe discovered this centuries ago, summering in the mountains and then dropping into the snow-free canyon

A young Nez Perce dancer honoring his forefathers

Wallowa Band Nez Perce Trail Interpretive Center in Wallowa

All of Oregon is **beautiful**. But for my money, eastern Oregon is just a bit **closer to heaven** on Earth.

Canola field in bloom below Chief Joseph Mountain

Hells Canyon at Granite Falls, with Seven Devils Range towering overhead

Cottonwoods decked out in fall colors on the shore of Wallowa Lake

bottoms for the winter. Today, ranchers employ the same strategy, driving their livestock to winter pastures that are thousands of feet lower than summer grasslands.

Northeast Oregon is so rugged that it was one of the last places in the West to be explored and settled. Ironically, the inhospitable and forbidding landscape that turned away those early explorers is precisely what draws hikers, climbers and sightseers to Wallowa County today.

Still, we're well supplied with open spaces and mercifully short on urban congestion. Wallowa County doesn't have a single traffic light. That doesn't mean it's lacking in culture, though, because there are lots of down-home events to enjoy.

A celebration of cowboy culture during Chief Joseph Days

Herefords grazing on the Zumwalt Prairie near Enterprise

A Kiger mustang at its new home on a Wallowa ranch

An 1880s horse barn and snow-frosted Wallowa Mountains near Joseph

Prairie Creek in the Nez Perce "Land of the Winding Waters"

View from Zumwalt Prairie of moonrise over Seven Devils Mountains

Prickly pear cactus blooming on sheer rock wall in Hells Canyon

Our biggest bash is the annual Chief Joseph Days, which includes one of the top small rodeos in the nation. But the celebration mainly serves to honor the legendary Nez Perce leader who called his homeland "that beautiful valley of winding waters" and added, "I love that land more than all the rest of the world."

All of Oregon is beautiful. But for my money, eastern Oregon is just a bit closer to heaven on Earth. Moving to God's Country was the best decision Cathy and I ever made. ✴

137

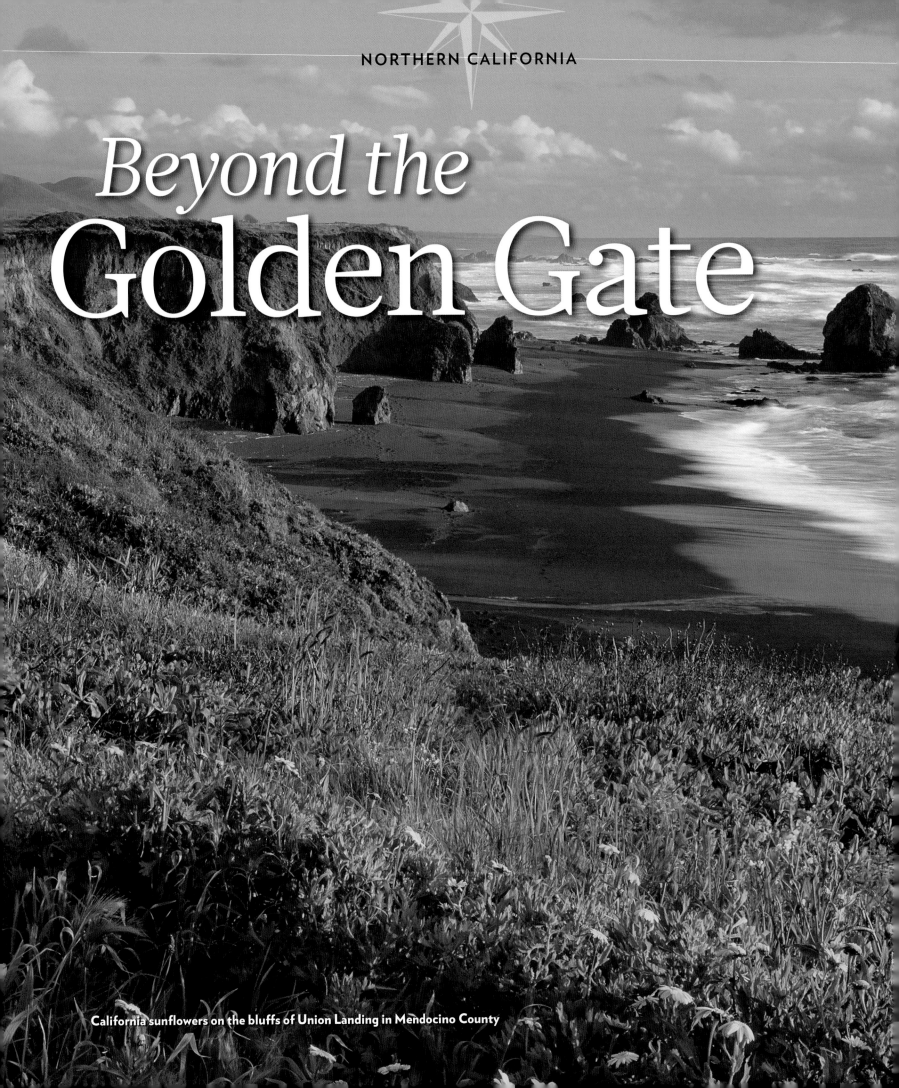

Beyond the Golden Gate

California sunflowers on the bluffs of Union Landing in Mendocino County

Explore ruggedly beautiful, richly historic Northern California.

Story by DONNA B. ULRICH • *Photos by* LARRY ULRICH

In many ways, the dividing line between Northern and Southern California is more a state of mind than a physical boundary. Southern California is about how people fit in with other people. Northern California is about how people fit into the land and how the land shapes us.

The northern half of our state attracts people who want to live in a beautiful, uncrowded place, put down roots and get things done. Up here, we're just more comfortable where trees outnumber people and rivers outnumber cities.

Opinions vary, but if they put me in charge of drawing the line between North and South, it would run from the San Francisco Bay area to Lake Tahoe. Then I'd draw a notch south along the Sierra Nevada to add Yosemite.

I have deep roots here; my grandmother grew up near Manchester, in Mendocino County. My mother often told the story of how my grandmother almost drowned when she was a girl. Grandma was returning from a trip on an ocean schooner when the small skiff ferrying her from ship to shore overturned.

A man passing by on the beach pulled her from the surf and saved her life, resuscitating her by rolling her back and forth over a barrel.

My twin sister and I spent summers on our aunt and uncle's farm in Suisun, cutting apricots for drying and picking prunes alongside my cousins.

Fresh eggs, veggies and all the apricots I could eat gave me a connection to the earth that living in the city could not. When

139

Surfnet fishing in Luffenholtz Beach County Park (right)

Colorful woolly lasthenia and Douglas iris (below right) in Gualala Point County Park

Fly-fishing on the Tuolumne River in Yosemite National Park (opposite)

I met Larry and had the chance to move away from the city to Humboldt County, it was an easy choice.

Larry grew up in the then-small East Bay town of Castro Valley, fishing and exploring the wild places in the Sierra Nevada with his father, a native Alaskan. Always in pursuit of the least crowded fishing holes, they hiked to alpine lakes and remote canyons on rivers named Stanislaus, Tuolumne, American, Feather and Pit.

But the family favorite was their campsite on the north fork of the Yuba River near the tiny town of Downieville. This past fall we stopped at the Yuba River, where Larry and his family spent their vacation each summer. Their old campsite was still there, including the flat place he and his brother Bob scraped out of the rocks for their tent.

So it was fitting that Larry proposed to me on a snowy evening in front of a blazing fire—on the trout farm where he caught his very first fish as a 4-year-old.

Rivers are the lifeblood of Northern California; these arteries used to teem with wild salmon and steelhead. But the Smith River in the northwestern corner is our last free-flowing river. The Eel, Trinity and Klamath rivers were also once famous for

The roots of our **family heritage** are anchored deep in the soil and rivers of **Northern California**.

Riverbank lupines in Humboldt County's Redwood Creek Valley

Unique sandstone concretions on Bowling Ball Beach near Schooner Gulch

their salmon spawning grounds, now depleted. The Sacramento River, Big Daddy of them all, drains rainwater from the Cascade and Coast ranges and the northern Sierra Nevada, finally running out into the delta and San Francisco Bay.

Water issues have bedeviled the state for more than a century. We have most of the water; the south has most of the people who want it. Northern Californians, who have always felt underrepresented in state government, even attempted in the early 1940s to join with southwestern Oregon to form a new state called Jefferson.

But it was the discovery of gold at Sutter's Mill on the American River in 1848 that shaped the region's history more than any other single event. Once the mad scramble for wealth began, there was no looking back. Oceans, mountains, forests and native tribes were simply obstacles to overcome on the way to riches.

San Francisco was transformed from a remote little port town to a booming city almost overnight. Lumber barons bought up vast virgin redwood forests, stretching from the Oregon border to south of San Francisco, and made fortunes logging them off. Today, only 4 percent of those forests remain—all of it protected in national or state parks.

Larry and I live in Humboldt County, a half-hour's drive from Redwood National Park. We spent so many days hiking its trails and taking photographs that we called it "the office."

To San Francisco's east, wine country anchors the southern end of Northern California, and a fine job it does. World-renowned Napa Valley vineyards put California on the map,

Neap tide at Houda Point Beach in Humboldt County

View of Camel Rocks from Luffenholtz Beach County Park in Trinidad

and now upstart vintners in Humboldt, Sonoma, Amador and Placer counties are helping maintain our reputation as a premium wine-producing region.

The Klamath Mountains bioregion makes up a major portion of northwestern California. The dramatic granite peaks of the Trinity Alps in Siskiyou County are perhaps the best known of the northern ranges. But the Marble Mountains to the north (with more than 150 documented caves), the Siskiyous to the west and the Salmons to the east also provide thousands of miles of scenic hiking trails that attract outdoor enthusiasts from all over the world.

From our home in Trinidad, we can reach dozens of wilderness trailheads in less than four hours, and we've backpacked many of them. Unusual flowers, a variety of orchids and lilies, and rare species of conifers offer botanists a field day. As the author of three books on wildflowers, Larry is always yearning to get back to the diverse flora and fauna of the region.

Grasslands once prevailed in the Central Valley, but today most of the land is used for farms and ranches. The vast herds of native antelope and elk are gone, but vernal pools and native grasslands remain in a few protected areas. Each fall, huge flocks of geese and ducks migrate to the Sacramento National Wildlife Refuge Complex, a habitat for more than 40 percent of the Pacific Flyway's wintering waterfowl.

North of the vast Central Valley, mountains once again take over. To the northeast, two volcanoes tower over the southern terminus of the Cascade Range. At 14,179 feet, Mount Shasta soars nearly 10,000 feet above the surrounding terrain. Lassen Peak, the other volcano, is the southernmost active volcano in the Cascades. On May 22, 1915, a powerful eruption devastated nearby areas and rained ash as far as 200 miles away.

Larry and I remember Lassen Peak for an event that's almost as rare around here: We were camping with friends in a remote section of Lassen Volcanic National Park when a strange light appeared in the night sky. We regarded one another with quizzical looks. Then, almost in unison, we asked, "Do you

Sonoma County vineyard decked out in fall colors

see what I see?" It was the eerie, pulsating light of the aurora borealis, the northern lights.

McCloud River, much of it owned by the Nature Conservancy, is one of the many clear streams that drain these rich volcanic lands. Burney Falls, a great place to photograph, is the most spectacular waterfall on this section of the Cascades. The water comes roaring over the face of the falls from underground springs, creating a cloud of cool mist that's a wonderful respite from the summer heat.

Farther south, the Sierra Nevada range takes over as the backbone of the eastern part of northern California. This is where you'll find Lake Tahoe, gem of gems, and Yosemite National Park, John Muir's heaven on Earth.

Larry and I are lucky to have traveled to so many beautiful places in our lives, places that make us remember and smile. But those places are other people's God's Country.

The roots of our family heritage are anchored deep in the soil and rivers of Northern California. Every time we return from our photographic travels, we're thankful to be back in the place that has given us so much. When we head north across the Golden Gate Bridge, or ascend the Sierra Nevada into the Central Valley, or leave the heat of the Cascades for the cool, foggy shadows of the redwood forests, we breathe a satisfied sigh. We're home in our God's Country. ✳

Bodie State Historic Park, a gold-rush ghost town in the Sierra Nevada

Trinidad Memorial Lighthouse on Trinidad Bay

Giant sequoias in Yosemite's Upper Mariposa Grove

Beloved Yosemite Chapel, oldest structure in Yosemite National Park

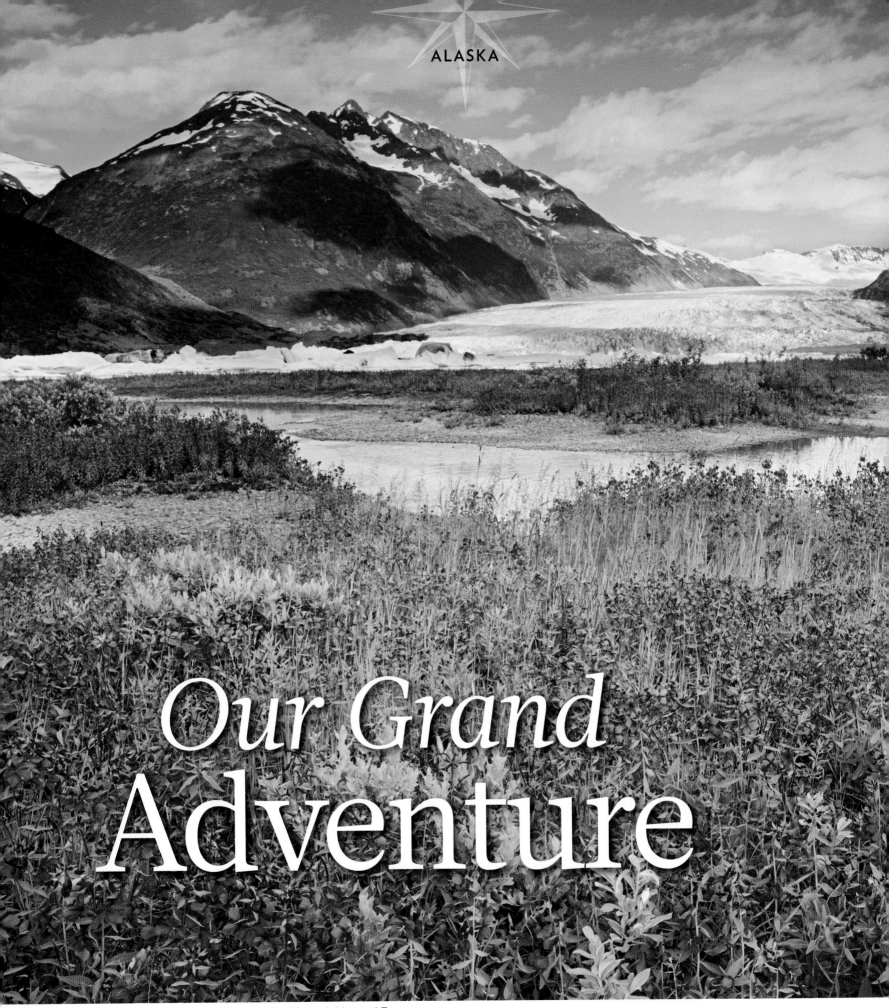

Our Grand Adventure

Wildflowers below Spencer Glacier in the Chugach National Forest

Alaska's untamed majesty brings out the explorer in us all.

Story by JANINE NIEBRUGGE • *Photos by* RON NIEBRUGGE

As my plane makes its approach into Anchorage, I look below to the rugged, snowcapped mountains of Chugach National Forest and its expansive ice fields and tidewater glaciers spilling into the fjords of Prince William Sound. This vast, untamed wilderness humbles me. Welcome to Alaska, the last frontier.

I was born and raised in Southern California. My husband, Ron, and I moved to Alaska 22 years ago. After a decade here, we left our office jobs to pursue his dream of working as a full-time professional photographer. Most of our friends thought we were crazy, but off we went and never looked back.

The gentle beauty of Alaska will steal your heart, from the lush rainforests in the southeast and along the coast to the barren tundra of the north. People who have been here are eager to share stories filled with fond memories and their wishes to return.

Alaska seems to encourage an outside-the-box attitude in its residents, or maybe people with that attitude are attracted to living here. Life here is not without challenges—in fact it is full of them—but these battles with nature make me feel more alive. The land is filled with energy, even though much of the state is uninhabited and untouched by humans.

Helicopters and kayaks are two of many favorite ways to explore Alaska, so when Ron suggested on a recent summer morning that we charter a helicopter to fly us to a remote glacial lake to kayak and take photos, I quickly agreed.

149

To truly **feel Alaska** in your heart you must immerse yourself in its **land and waters**.

Quiet pond below Mount Alice in the central Kenai Mountains (left)

Pedersen Glacier on Aialik Bay in Kenai Fjords National Park (below)

Spectacular display of northern lights over Seward harbor (opposite)

Our destination was Bear Glacier Lagoon in Kenai Fjords National Park. On the way we flew over the expansive Harding Ice Field and then to Aialik Bay so Ron could capture some photos of Aialik and Holgate glaciers. We then followed Bear Glacier to the lagoon.

Alaska's beauty and vastness are best appreciated from the air. But to truly feel Alaska in your heart you must immerse yourself in its land and waters. As I kayaked among mammoth icebergs, some the size of high-rise buildings, I felt free and at peace in this private moment, quiet except for the occasional snap-crackle-pop as a chunk of glacier broke free and calved into the water.

The seasons set the rhythm of our lives here. We live much like the bears that share our wilderness—hibernating in winter and working and playing like mad in summer.

In some areas of Alaska, the sun never rises for several months. At our home on the shores of Resurrection Bay, we have about four hours of daylight on the shortest days of winter. The landscape is mostly gray and white, sprinkled with bursts of color when we see a dramatic winter sunrise or a brilliant display of the northern lights.

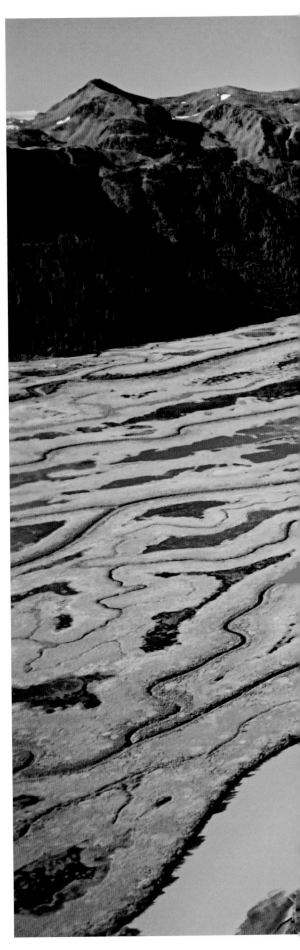

Brief burst of brilliant fall color in Denali National Park

Verdant Copper River delta in the Chugach National Forest

A regal bald eagle and chicks in their nest

Dog sledding on Punch Bowl Glacier near Girdwood

Bull caribou in Denali National Park

Sea otter and her adorable pup on Prince William Sound's Orca Inlet

154

Bull moose browsing below Mount McKinley in Denali National Park

Of course, limited daylight doesn't stop Alaskans from getting out and snowshoeing, hiking, skiing or riding snow machines. A perfect winter day for me involves a hike through the forest after a fresh snow, when songbirds sing from sleeping trees and sunbeams stream through the dense forest. Winter is a time for rest and reflection, a chance to recharge our batteries for the busy summer season that will soon be upon us. The quiet sound of gently falling snow is food for the soul.

As winter gives way to spring, the snow melts and trees come alive as buds burst open. A brilliant emerald green color blankets the mountainsides and valleys. Soon colorful wildflowers begin to dot the landscape.

Summer in Alaska is short and we take full advantage of the long daylight hours. A subsistence lifestyle is still practiced by many here, not just those in rural communities but in cities as well. It's essential to stock the freezer with fish and game during summer and to build up the woodpile.

Endless possibilities for adventure exist for both visitors and

Childs Glacier spectacularly calving into the Copper River near Cordova

Back-country snowboarding in Chugach National Forest

locals—from whale-watching cruises to river rafting, or even taking a helicopter to a sled dog camp.

Autumn in Alaska is fleeting, and my favorite place to experience its splendor is Denali National Park. Birch and aspen trees turn a brilliant yellow, and the rolling tundra hills burst into vivid shades of red, magenta and orange.

I never tire of witnessing this colorful display and always have the same reaction: God must be an artist and the landscape is his canvas. Alaska's wildlife looks magnificent at this time of year, plump and sporting glossy new fur coats. The pace of living begins to slow as our transition to winter begins again.

I had no idea about the grand adventure that awaited me when we arrived in Alaska. On any given day I can look out our living room window and see bald eagles, humpback whales, sea otters and sea lions. Even the occasional moose has strolled through our front yard.

Across the bay, the first thing I see every morning is Mount Alice rising from the Chugach National Forest. This peak has been the backdrop for many stunning sunrises and has even played host to dancing displays of northern lights. Remarkable scenery and a generous, warm-hearted community surround us. If this isn't God's Country, then I don't know what is! ✳

Contributors

Mary Liz Austin

Mary Liz Austin is a professional landscape photographer who strives to create an intimate relationship with her subject. She travels the United States searching for scenes that depict quintessential Americana and the magnificence and beauty of our national lands. She is proficient in both large-format and digital media, and her work is featured in countless books, calendars and magazines. Her images and stories have graced *Country* for 16 years. Mary Liz lives and works on Vashon Island, Washington, with her husband, Terry Donnelly.

Pat & Chuck Blackley

Pat and Chuck Blackley are a photography and writing team born and raised in Virginia. Although they work throughout North America, their concentration is on the eastern United States. With a love of history, they find a wealth of subjects in the mid-Atlantic. Books include *Shenandoah National Park Impressions*, *Blue Ridge Parkway Impressions*, *Shenandoah Valley Impressions*, *Outer Banks Impressions*, *Backroads From the Beltway*, *Our Virginia*, *Blue Ridge Parkway Simply Beautiful* and *Virginia's Historic Homes and Gardens*.

Terry Donnelly

Terry Donnelly is an award-winning landscape and nature photographer. His images have appeared in Reiman Media Group publications, including *Country*, since 1988. "My greatest joy in photography is engaging the challenge of interpreting the beauty of nature in new, meaningful ways." Terry's photography has been featured in many books, magazines and calendars, and he has six large-format books to his credit. He also enjoys teaching photography. He lives and works with his wife, Mary Liz Austin, on Vashon Island, Washington.

Kenny Dunn

Kenny Dunn grew up in a family that enjoyed camping, fishing and other outdoor adventures. His grandfather, a photography enthusiast, gave him a professional camera system and a freezer full of film when he was a kid. "Photography has made me seek out the most beautiful places in the country at the most spectacular times." His favorite subjects are in his backyard: places like Red River Gorge or Cumberland Gap in Kentucky. When not behind the camera, he is often on his mountain bike or motorcycle, or spending time with his family.

Bob Firth

Bob Firth is a stock and assignment photographer in Chaska, Minnesota, who has spent more than 35 years photographing the great outdoors. Bob combines his passion for photography with sports and his leadership as an outdoor educator. He has more than 2 million images available through Firth PhotoBank. His images have been on the covers of more than 300 magazines, countless calendar pages and in books including *Landscape of Ghosts* by Bill Holm, *The Gift of Time*, *Minneapolis & St. Paul: A Photographic Portrait*, *The Superior North Shore*, and more.

Joe & Becky Gibbons

Joe and Becky Gibbons have been chasing radiant light for 15 years, always in search of the next inspiring photograph. They are especially drawn to capture the overlooked landscapes of the southeastern United States. From the salty air of Florida's coast to the hazy blue mountains of the Carolinas, their quest to capture America's beauty is a never-ending passion in their journey of life. Though they are based in central Florida, they are constantly on the move and traveling across the countryside to find their next great shot.

Mike Grandmaison

Mike Grandmaison is regarded as one of Canada's finest nature photographers. Published worldwide in books, calendars and magazines (including *Country*), Mike is at home in the natural world of his beloved country, Canada. He has written 10 books including *Mike Grandmaison's Prairie and Beyond*, *Muskoka*, *Georgian Bay*, *The Canadian Rockies* and *Canada*. Mike has contributed a regular feature in *Outdoor Photography Canada* magazine called "Discovering Canada" since 2007. Mike lives in Winnipeg, Manitoba, in the heart of the North American continent.

Russell Graves

Ever since he can remember, Russell Graves has been fascinated with nature, wildlife, agriculture and the outdoors. "As a teenager on my family's cattle ranch, I recall being chastised for searching for deer when I was supposed to be looking for lost cattle in the hardwood bottomlands that filter the muddy waters of Bois d'Arc Creek. I went to school in the tiny northeast Texas town of Dodd City, where I was surrounded by a rural culture that is still strong. Because of my background as a small town guy, I feel I bring a fresh perspective to my photography and writing that makes my work unique."

Jerry Irwin

Jerry Irwin has been a full-time photographer since 1974, and before that he snapped photos as a hobby. He has published nine books on topics including Pennsylvania, Philadelphia, barns, the Amish and motorcycles. His images have appeared in *National Geographic*, *Life*, *The Saturday Evening Post*, *Sports Illustrated*, *Country* and *Farm & Ranch Living*. Jerry is a four-time winner in the Nikon Photo Contest International, including the gold medal. He has also completed four digital books on Blurb.com.

David Jensen

David Jensen has been a professional photographer for nearly 40 years. His photos have appeared in many national publications including books by *National Geographic* and Time-Life, magazines like *Sierra*, *Natural History*, *Country*, *Popular Photography* and *Outdoor Photographer*, and also calendars. His photo library includes tens of thousands of images of eastern Oregon and other Western states. Reiman Media Group began using his images in the 1980s. He lives with his wife, Cathy, in Enterprise, Oregon.

Greg Latza

A former farm boy, Greg Latza is a freelance corporate and editorial photographer whose work centers around the Great Plains and its rich mix of people. Primarily a contract photographer, Greg cherishes any chance he gets to head off on his own and travel America's backroads. Greg maintains a diverse fine art catalog of country, rural and agricultural images. An accomplished author, Greg and his wife, Jodi, have produced nine books of photography that cover their home state of South Dakota.

Janine & Ron Niebrugge

Alaska-based professional photographer Ron Niebrugge is most at home in the wilderness. Taking the ordinary and using natural light to create the extraordinary has been a passion of Ron's for many years. Ron's images have caught the attention of many and he is pleased to have among his clients *National Geographic*, *Sports Illustrated*, Walt Disney World, Continental Airlines, Alaska Airlines and the National Park Service, to name a few. Ron and his wife, Janine, operate a stock photography business in Seward, Alaska.

Robert Olejniczak

An avid outdoorsman, Robert Olejniczak enjoys sharing his love of nature with others through his photography. He calls western New York home, where he lives with his wife and writing partner, Nancy, and their two children. He looks forward to retiring from his full-time job as a mail carrier so that he can spend more time exploring and capturing the beauty of God's Country with his camera. His photography work has been published in *Country* and other Reiman publications since 1993.

Gary Rasmussen

Gary Rasmussen is a part-time photographer specializing in the landscapes of the Southwest. Gary is a biologist and lives in Albuquerque, where he does contract compliance work for the Department of Defense and NASA. Gary's images have been published since 1985 in a variety of books, fine art prints, calendars, postcards, posters, magazines and screen savers in both the United States and Canada. He has worked for many publishers including Reiman Media Group, as well as The Wildlife Society and The Nature Conservancy.

John Sylvester

Award-winning author and photographer John Sylvester lives on Prince Edward Island, Canada. Although he travels extensively in North America and abroad, he is continually drawn back to the distinctive coastal landscape and communities of Canada's Atlantic provinces, especially Newfoundland & Labrador. "It's a place that never fails to surprise and reward me with great images and wonderful experiences." John is the author of several books and his photography appears in leading publications throughout the world, including *Country*.

Donna & Larry Ulrich

Larry Ulrich has been making a living with a sharp eye for the beauty and soul of this country for 40 years, first with a 4x5 film camera and now with a digital Nikon system. He and his wife, Donna, have worked as field editors for *Country* magazine for much of that time, Larry with his photos and Donna with her words. They run a little agency, marketing to such icons as the Sierra Club, National Audubon Society and *National Geographic*, and have taken enough calendar shots to fill the Grand Canyon. Larry and Donna live in Trinidad, on California's northern coast.

"Keep close to Nature's heart…and break clear away, once in a while, and climb a mountain or spend a week in the woods. Wash your spirit clean."

John Muir

Half Moon Arch in Red River Gorge, Kentucky   PHOTO BY KENNY DUNN